THE ORPHAN DREAMER

THE ORPHAN DREAMER

An insightful tale offering hope and purpose
in a restless world.

AARON BROWN

THE ORPHAN DREAMER. Copyright © 2023 by Aaron Brown

All rights reserved. Printed in the United States of America.

This is a work of fiction. Names, characters, places, and incidents are either the product of the author's imagination or are used fictitiously. Any resemblance to actual events, locales, or persons, living or dead, is coincidental.

No part of this book may be reproduced, or stored in a retrieval system, or transmitted in any form or by any means, electronic, mechanical, photocopying, recording, or otherwise, without express written permission of the publisher.

Library of Congress Control Number: 2023921616

ISBN: 9798867035495

To my charming wife,
Andrea,

To my enchanting daughters,
Avery and Sophia,

To those who are thirsty
for hope and purpose,

And to all wrestling
with a longing for more.

ONE

A third blood-stained tissue fell to the floor, landing near the others.

An hour earlier, the orphan's arms were pinned behind his back by a heavyset kid, while another punched him twice in the face. He used to tell the clergy about the bullying, but now he resisted. It mattered little if he told them, for he was generally blamed when others harassed him.

All he ever knew was the convent. Abandoned by his parents as a baby, the monastery took him in until he might be adopted. But adoption never came; the large birthmark spanning the left side of his face alarmed most people at first sight. And the fact that the blemish resembled an unruly-looking *X* didn't help. His parents believed it to be an ominous warning of troubling things to come for any associated with the boy. And though he behaved quite well, every time promising parents toured the campus, they routinely selected another child.

While his basic necessities of food and shelter were provided, his fundamental need for love and affection was altogether missing. He was treated poorly by those in authority and teased by the other children in the house. Sometimes he wished it would all just end.

His nose finally stopped bleeding, and the the boy jotted a few notes into his notebook. He had longed to write a book for some time, but always lacked inspiration for a compelling story. He absolutely adored books. Volume upon volume, he could escape present circumstances and transcend to far away places. He could travel and be whomever he wished, wealthy or poor, famous or nameless. Setting his pen and notebook upon the nightstand, beneath the glow of the moon penetrating the far window, the young aspiring writer drifted anxiously to sleep.

Suddenly, the boy knew he was dreaming. He felt at once fully alert and simultaneously unconscious as he slumbered. He observed himself being transported somewhere into Mexico and lured deep within a dark cavern. A ray of sunlight filtered down through the rocky abyss. Before him emerged a pool of water, sparkling and crystal clear. The cavernous pond, though miniature in size, boasted healing qualities for any affliction. He could at last be restored from the reckless birthmark that plagued his face. Longing to be free from this burden continually weighing him down, the boy stepped into the watery abyss. It was cool and refreshing. He slowly slipped into the depths until wholly submerged. Upon rising to the surface, an unrecognizable joy and newness of life overwhelmed him. A flood of euphoria surged from within his soul and heightened his senses as he withdrew from the pool.

Retreating from the murky cavern, he noticed three Spanish ships far in the distance, anchored along the shoreline. Each was ablaze with fire, black smoke wafting upward into a bright, blue sky. As his eyes beheld the radiant sun, it was then the boy promptly awoke from the dream.

It seemed so real, he mused. So lifelike. Why would he have such a dream, and why was the ending so random? Three ships billowing with smoke; what could it mean? What if there *was* a healing pool able to restore his face and remove his unsightly blemish? He would be normal, like everyone else. They wouldn't stare; they wouldn't laugh. People would accept him. Maybe, even love him.

After breakfast, all the orphans met for morning chapel, where the priest shared a brief story from the Bible. He spoke on the numerous ancient gates along the walls of Jerusalem, each serving a distinct function. One was named the Sheep Gate, and near it was a pool of water surrounded by five porches. Upon each porch lay a great number of people who were sick, paralyzed, blind, or lame, all awaiting the angel. For they knew that an angel would descend into the pool at a certain time to stir up the water. And whoever stepped in first after the stirring of the water would be healed of his disease or disorder.

The boy with the dream listened attentively. Was this account a coincidence on the very same morning as his own night vision? Or could it be fate? Perhaps an angel had spoken directly to him. "Does the healing pool still exist today?" the dreamer asked aloud.

"Not that we know of," replied the priest with a smirk. "Sorry, son. Your face will always look like that." The room erupted as the other children laughed hysterically. The priest stretched out his arm with an open palm toward the boy. "You were a mistake, it's true, and the birthmark clearly confirms it." he continued. Giggling lingered with all eyes staring at the orphan. "Life is not always fair, I'm afraid," the priest lamented.

The priest resumed his lecture. "Just as the angel purified the water for healing, so too does fire, a purifier and refiner of the soul. God assigns many tests over the course of our lifetime in order to purify and burn away the dross of sin, that our soul might be perfected." Maybe that's what the burning ships represented in the dream? the boy considered.

It oddly began to smell like smoke. In the rear of the chapel, an orphan who rarely ever spoke, had lit a wooden toy boat on fire. Grasping the bottom of the boat, he gently moved it up and down before him as if it was floating upon the waves of the sea. The dreamer turned in his seat to witness this strange occurrence, flames licking excitedly and sending smoke drifting into the air. The orphan clutching the boat said nothing and simply stared at the boy with the birthmark.

"Take him to the closet!" ordered the priest to the nuns in the sanctuary. They dragged the silent orphan with the fiery boat away once again, as he often misbehaved for the sake of needed attention. Favoritism was undeniable within the convent, as most of the children were poorly treated. It all depended if they liked you or not, and if not, you likely spent time in locked closets or were forced to stand for hours while holding your arms straight out. Some were beaten, even shaken into shock, and one unfortunate girl was shoved down the stairs for failing to follow precise orders.

The dreamer decided to tell no one about his dream. They would only laugh and tease him. Instead, it would remain his secret to ponder in his heart.

That evening, he slid into a deep sleep and again dreamed of a mysterious cavern, a shimmering healing pool, and three ancient Galleon ships burning in the distance. Gazing into the golden Mexican sun once more, he was immediately awakened as before.

He knew he must leave. His conscience was prompting him to step out, urging him to follow this new calling. What the boy desired most, more than anything in the world, was to be healed of his disfigurement—to be like everyone else. He knew it was vain, no question there, for he enjoyed good health, and scores of people suffered conditions far worse. But he was inspired nonetheless.

He reflected on his years living in the convent and the manner in which he was treated. In all fairness, he was not truly an orphan as most of the other children. Many had lost their parents due to some manner of death. But he was actually a foundling, abandoned and unwanted by his living parents, unwanted for the sake of a crudely distorted birthmark in the shape of an *X*, stamped as defective and unacceptable. Nobody harassed a child for losing her parents from an early passing. But where does one find confidence and discover his true identity when disowned by able parents?

His fate was up to him, the boy reasoned. He had wanted to run away for some time but feared the limited opportunity awaiting him at such a youthful age. Even now at fifteen, who would hire him to work and how would he provide for himself?

Forever fearful of strangers and taking risks, that was all going to change. He was emboldened by his recent dreams and apparent confirmations encouraging him to pursue them.

I don't need the convent, he bitterly assured himself. I don't need the church either—they're full of hypocrites! And I don't need God.

Tonight's the night, he decided. It will all be fine. "We each choose our own destiny," he whispered to himself.

After dinner, the boy withdrew from the dining hall alone to prepare for his escape. Prior to reaching the corridor leading to his room, the heavy-set bully sprang from around a corner and tripped him. The boy floundered a few feet before flopping upon the floor in a heap. He paused there a moment to regain his bearings. The cold tile beneath his palms was reminiscent of the hostile environment in the convent, he noticed.

"You gonna get up, you weirdo?" the bully jeered. His friend laughed smugly, "Just stay down; it's where you belong!"

The boy remained silent and composed as he gingerly rose to his feet. Then, turning around, he suddenly charged toward his foe at full speed. He didn't care. So what if he got in trouble? But in the last moment, the bully ducked to the side. And clutching the boy's shirt as he sailed by, he shoved him into the wall head on. The orphan's head bounced off the wall with a deep thud and he collapsed to the floor.

TWO

The orphan snuck down the long hallway in his socks while carrying a hefty backpack on his shoulders. It was late in the night and all were sleeping. Unlocking the side entrance, he glanced back for one last look. This had been his home his entire life, and while there were good times dotted along the way, they were few and far between. He wouldn't miss the cruel discipline and relentless abuse and oppression from his peers.

Outside was chilly. He was thankful that he piled on several layers of clothing. Better to be warm and able to remove clothes than miserably cold and helpless. He slid his shoes on and quietly fled the property. The bus station was not far, and he knew exactly how to get there.

He was grateful for the little secrets he had gleaned over the years at the convent. Once, while being scolded in the office, the boy caught a glimpse of a small wad of cash stashed inside one of the desk drawers. Aware the office often remained unlocked during the day, he had conveniently snuck in to borrow the money for his present journey.

Okay, he knew he had no plans of returning the money, but he had never stolen anything before. It was difficult to accept the fact that he had just done so, and thus he justified that he would merely borrow the cash—indefinitely. He needed it for food and for bus and train tickets, and besides, they owed him for years of mistreatment. That was the least he deserved!

The orphan was surprised how cold he was considering the amount of clothing he was wearing. New England can be a cold and dark place, he thought. Even with the breeze, a thick silence surrounded him with leafless trees and lifeless streets. He reached the bus station late into the night, a closed sign hanging loosely upon the glass door.

A solitary moth was flying around an outdoor canopy light. It persistently bumped into the light fixture and bounced away, only to circle and do the same over and over again. That always intrigued the lad, as to why they would never learn and simply do something else. Some insects love the darkness, he noted. The cockroach emerges in the evening but scurries toward dark spaces whenever light emits. But moths were different. They were nocturnal, appearing primarily at night, but were actually attracted to sources of light.

Maybe humans were similar to insects, he wondered. Many love the darkness as the cockroach and shun light and truth entirely. Others dwell in the dark as moths, but they seek light and some level of truth in the world. Moths often wander back into sheer darkness, but they generally return to the light source that initially attracted them. Perhaps these are like people who lack faith, convinced of little, and yet continue to return in search of truth.

The boy's attention shifted toward a homeless man sitting on the sidewalk in front of the bus station, clutching a bottle of liquor. Hopelessness and gloom weighed heavily as confusion set in. What am I doing? the orphan challenged himself. Maybe I should turn back. I could make it back before anyone knew that I left.

"Life's not fair!" cried the man without a home, in the direction of the boy.

The boy was startled. "Have you no place to stay?"

"Been out here for years, making it on my own, doing it *my* way!" he blurted. "Hey, what happened to your face?"

"Just a birthmark, no big deal," the boy replied, not wanting to talk about it. "Where's your family?" asked the boy, wishing to change the subject. "Can't they help you?"

"My family won't help; they think I'm lazy," the man bitterly replied. "Won't give me any money—and they have plenty to spare, I tell you!"

The orphan wanted to walk away but didn't want to seem rude. "Why not get a job? Lots of places are hiring right now. I see signs everywhere."

The man grew irritable. "Because the whole system is rigged! There's no chance for someone like me." He drew the bottle to his mouth and drank generously. "Life is not fair," he moaned again, much more calmly. "Life's not fair," he echoed.

The boy walked down a bit, just shy of the overhead lights, and lay down on his side upon the pavement. He zipped up his jacket around a hooded sweatshirt and contemplated the man without a home. He's entirely fit to work, and yet chooses otherwise. It's his own choice.

He eyed the man down aways drawing another drink. He's right, life is *not* fair—for anyone. Everyone is struggling with something on some level. It must be easier to get through difficult times for people who accept this as part of life. But each of us is faced with a choice. We always have a choice, he assured himself. He recalled a book he had read while at the convent, reinforcing that what matters is what you do with today. It stressed establishing a habit every morning in order to succeed, even if it was simply making your bed. It argued that it's the smallest of details that matter. If only the homeless man would ask what small act he could accomplish today to make this day count for something. And then he could build upon that, little by little, and take initiative. Why, the homeless man could change the world if he so wanted!

Rolling onto his back, the orphan sighed and gazed into the night sky above. His eyes were promptly drawn to the Orion constellation. Familiar with many star patterns, Orion was his favorite and generally the easiest to recognize on a cloudless night. Resembling a hunter bearing both sword and shield, Orion always fascinated the boy. Three stars formed the hunter's belt, and they shined so brightly it was difficult to miss. He learned in church that even the Bible mentions Orion on three separate occasions. "He is the maker of the Bear and Orion," he recalled one scripture. That was written thousands of years ago, he considered. Stars are so constant and predictable, just hovering in space unmoved. Early mankind admired the exact same stars as he this evening.

The great Hunter, he continued to stare in wonder. We are all hunting in a way, the orphan thought. We are each searching for something: for more in life, for meaning, for purpose. I must believe in my dreams, no matter how big they seem. They say most people will laugh when someone pursues an unusual vision. But you have to believe. I have a dream that I must follow. I must embrace it for it is my own. And even if I fail, at

THE ORPHAN DREAMER

least I gave it a shot. If I never try, I will never fail, it is certain, but new ideas and opportunities will forever remain foreign to me. There is a danger, he supposed, in neither stepping out in trying nor using caution in so doing. I must use discernment in taking calculated risks.

I am now more alone and isolated than ever before, he concluded. And yet, I am free to alter the course of my life.

THREE

People arrived at the bus station early in the morning, with little regard for the two homeless gentlemen out front. One remained snoring, subconsciously gripping his bottle of booze; the other hurriedly arose and grabbed his backpack. He dashed across the street and up a block to a diner just opening, and ordered two meals to go. Returning to the bus station, he set one meal next to the sleeping homeless man, and then carried his own breakfast inside the station.

After purchasing a map at the counter, he bought one bus ticket south to New York City. It would leave in a couple of hours and arrive in the Big Apple later that evening. He was on his way.

༄

As he took his seat near the back of the bus, the orphan noticed something protruding from in-between the seat and the back seat rest. He pulled it out—a crisp twenty dollar bill! He examined the money while sitting down, mouth halfway open. Was it chance the bill was in the seat he just happened to pick? He remembered what they had taught at the convent: give and it shall be given to you.

Could it be true? Was it a reflection of the meal he purchased for the homeless man hours prior? If so, karma must be real. And that's one thing he never understood. If karma is, in fact, a valid concept, then what is influencing the allotment for good or bad outcomes to occur? If the universe is not a living entity, with the ability to think and reason as a person, does that imply there is some manner of higher Being who is both blessing and cursing humanity depending upon their deeds?

The boy examined the money again. If the more I hand out, the more I get back, then I should give away as much as I possibly can. I would be a fool to do otherwise! But something told him it probably doesn't work that way, for that would be giving from greed, for selfish gain instead of kindness. The motive in giving must be pure, he decided.

As the bus pulled away, the boy watched the trees move faster and faster. He likely would never again see any of these trees, or the area for that matter. Not only was he traveling outside his comfort zone, but he was headed for a different country altogether. Taking the risk in setting out, especially with so little, one never knew what awaited around the next corner: new experiences, people, places, and fresh challenges and opportunities. Many dangers may well await him and plenty of hurdles ahead for sure, but life was exciting now. Life was suddenly interesting and hopeful.

A handful of people crawled onto the bus at the following stop. A blind woman meandered down the center aisle and tactfully felt around the seat across from the boy. Perceiving an empty seat, she carefully sat down and set her cane against the wall of the bus. "What a gorgeous day indeed!" she exclaimed with a genuine smile.

"Forgive me for asking," the orphan took the bait, with furrowed brow. "But how do you know?"

"Oh my, can't you sense it, the warmth?" the woman asked. "I feel the sunshine on my face, not too many clouds today. And the brightness of the morning is delightful," she said while circling her hands in the air. "Before getting on the bus, I heard children laughing and birds chattering. And you can't deny the scent of maple in the air and the hints of apple. I love the smells in this part of the country."

"Wow, I'm impressed!" replied the boy, genuinely in awe.

"What, you thought because I'm blind I lacked any sense?" she said while laughing. "I may be blind, young man, but I can surely see."

"I meant no disrespect," he tried to recover. "It's just that you are so joyful; it's refreshing."

"Honey, the more grateful you are, the greater the beauty you will witness all around you. Life will abound with goodness and your joy will flourish."

The boy was listening, but not convinced. She had no idea about his eccentric-looking birthmark traversing his face. "It's not always that easy. I have troubles you wouldn't understand." He leaned back in his seat and looked straight ahead.

"Don't focus on the seemingly bad," she persisted. "Discover the positive side of each circumstance in your life. You must remain optimistic. You will find yourself more content and productive than you could otherwise imagine."

Perhaps she's right, he thought. He had always been told to strive in being a better person—to read, to learn, to listen more while speaking less. "So you believe that good can come from the bad situations in one's life?"

"*Seemingly* bad situations, yes," she reiterated, while sliding closer to the aisle. "Listen to me, dear. My eyes have failed me. I'm unable to drive, so I ride the bus. But I steer the course of my life. I assume control of my own actions; I shape my behavior. Without sight I still retain my vision."

"But I've endured a lonely childhood," the orphan lamented with watery eyes. "The world is against me, and I can never seem to catch a break."

The woman without sight reached across the aisle and found the boy's hand. "Take my advice: be intentional about determining your future. Establish goals and a path in achieving them. Don't stress over achieving huge accomplishments. A person's destiny is conditioned by the sum of the smallest choices that he makes."

"You're probably right," he somewhat agreed. "For so long, I assumed that fate was already determined for a person. That little, if anything, could be done to alter its course."

"Take nothing for granted, dear boy. And listen for the signs —they're literally all around you. Be patient. Before you know it, something good your way will come."

The bus was pulling into New York City as the boy was waking up. Looking around, he noticed the blind woman was gone. He hopped off the bus and asked directions to the train station. It was close, less than a mile away. Once there, he purchased a train ticket and awaited the train's arrival.

I'm following my dreams, the boy assured himself with a grin. It matters little what others think of me. I will shape my own life, my own reality. Anything is possible.

FOUR

Boarding the train, the orphan grew self-conscious of his facial blemish. So many people were coming and going, and all were strangers. And while few people knew one another on the train, he was an outsider, an alien, in his mind. People stared at his birthmark when passing by, and though desperately trying to remain confident and indifferent regarding peer pressures, it was no use. He *did* care what people thought of him and longed to be accepted as any other. He wished he could slip on a mask while on the train.

Everyone wears a disguise anyway, he reasoned, a facade covering up their true selves, hoping to trick others into believing they are someone other than whom they really are. Strangers always stare when they meet him and criticize his face, whether silently or aloud. If only they saw his heart and all that he stood for; it was like judging a book by the cover without investing time to comprehend its contents. The very soul of the book and reason for its being, overlooked for lack of interest.

A well-dressed man sat next to the boy on the train. "Hey there, where you headed?" asked the man.

The boy hesitated while eyeing the newcomer. "Uh… Mexico," the boy reluctantly replied, almost as a question.

"Oh my, not sure if this train travels that far." He placed a leather briefcase on the floor below his seat.

"It doesn't, but I'll take it as far as I can," said the boy. "What about you?"

"I'm not going far. I get off at the City of Brotherly Love."

"Where is that?" the boy asked, suddenly hesitant about sitting near this man.

The man slung one leg over the other. "Don't you know? Philadelphia, of course!" he chuckled. "The name's Greek, meaning brotherly love. Interesting story: a man named William Penn envisioned a town where all religions would be welcome. No harassment would be allowed and peace would flourish with the native Americans in the area."

The boy squinted his eyes and pursed his lips to one side. "And how did that work out?"

"Not as well as Penn hoped, I imagine!" The man turned to peer down the aisle, and then faced the boy again. "You say you're going to Mexico? What's there?"

"I dreamed of a healing pool somewhere in Mexico." He figured he would never see this man again, so who cares if he laughs. "I plan to find it and have my face restored."

The well-dressed man perked up with intrigue and cleared his throat. "Ah, I see. Dreams are a mystery for sure. Certain truths are revealed to some by means of visions, while they remain concealed to others. Dreams are a link between the physical and spiritual worlds, like alternate dimensions. They're usually taken for granted—people often blame them on a meal they ate prior to bed.

"I urge you to listen to your dreams," the man continued. "At times, it is God whispering to your soul. Other times the conscience is intending to guide an individual or issue a warning, if only he will take heed." He looked off into space for a moment in reflection before reverting his attention back to the boy. "I've noticed that those who live morally tend to enjoy more wholesome dreams, while those living immorally suffer visions of rebuke and warning."

"How do you know so much about dreams?" inquired the orphan.

"I've been a therapist for many years, and during that time I've discerned a clear connection between dreams and consciousness. Most don't give them a second thought, but the relationship often serves as divine enlightenment to an individual."

A weight lifted from the orphan and a calmness filled its place. He was still unsure if he believed in God, but if these words were valid, then his soul likely heard from an Entity in another dimension. It made sense. Why else would we entertain dreams when asleep?

"I have witnessed numerous of my patients find healing," the therapist regressed. "Some ailments are more challenging than others, of course, but I am convinced that any manner of emotional distress or trauma may be cured if one recognizes the proper channel of treatment."

"So you believe I'll be healed?" the orphan asked with hope in his voice.

"Well, to be fair, most of my clients seek emotional or mental restoration," he clarified. "And even then, one might never forget his past, for adversity has a way of leaving a scar." The man studied the boy's face for signs of understanding. "But with time and suitable therapy, with forgiveness, time lends mercy and a promise of renewal." After pausing for a moment, he nodded his head as if agreeing with himself, and continued. "Forgiveness is key. Without it, much healing is hopeless—and yet, within arm's reach all the while."

"I'm not sure I can forgive some people from my past," the orphan stated defensively. "Some don't deserve forgiveness; some aren't even sorry for what they've done!"

"I understand where you're coming from," the therapist acknowledged. He uncrossed his legs and crossed them the other way. "Forgive them anyway. It's healthier for your mind and your thoughts. Set aside negativity and choose to be joyful. Be thankful no matter what, and you'll find it's easier to remain positive."

The boy sat quietly, mulling over the man's advice.

"I see you weighing my words. That's a good thing; you can never be too hasty. You possess the ability to think and reason, and you have an internal moral code to discern between right and wrong. Contemplate counsel and ideas until you are convinced one way or the other. And always make time for self-reflection. People need to get alone more often and resolve the moral dilemmas swimming around in their heads. That's how we grow."

"I just wish more people saw it that way," the boy sighed. He turned his head away from the therapist and looked out the window. Rolling hills wandered leisurely in the distance. "People can be so cruel."

"Be the change you want around you. Be the light you want to see in the world," added the well-dressed man. "People are forever filled with doubts. Believe in yourself, my friend—even when nobody else does."

FIVE

Philadelphia arrived swiftly and the therapist bid farewell before departing the train. The boy reflected on the man's wisdom. While still unsure if he was ready to forgive others for their wrongs trespassed against him, he felt encouraged. Healing was possible if he discovered the proper treatment. And he could be the change that he desired in others—he yearned to be different, to be a better person. He would commit to believing in himself, come what may; it matters not how others view him. Words do have power, he reasoned. The therapist chose his words wisely, using them for good. He, too, would strive to use words to inspire rather than for harm.

The train continued on its steady southerly course toward the District of Columbia. An hour later, the orphan felt a gentle rumble and tensing of his stomach. He had forgotten all about eating. The dining car was two railcars ahead, so he took a leisurely stroll toward the smell of food. On his way through the first car, several passengers stared at the boy with curiosity. That was the norm for him and he paid little attention. Upon reaching the dining car, he passed two teenage boys seated across from one another at a dining table. They were giggling upon his approach and one pointed directly at him. "What happened to your face, freak?" he cried out loudly. The other mockingly chimed in, "The circus is the other direction. Turn around and go back!"

The other diners continued eating and kept to themselves, pretending not to hear. But an older, polished man motioned to the boy from his seat several dining tables in the distance. He dressed comfortably in nice jeans and a polo shirt, but what caught the eye were his black rectangular glasses, sleek and refined. "Don't mind them," he insisted as the boy reached his table. "Insecure punks," he said with a quick glance in their direction. "Join me if you like," motioning with his hand to the empty chair across from him.

After they both ordered food, the man asked the boy if his parents were on the train. "No, I don't have any."

"Neither mother nor father?"

"No, neither," the orphan repeated himself.

He studied the boy carefully. "Brothers or sisters?"

"No, not that I'm aware of."

"All alone in the world. From where have you come?" he interrogated his new friend.

The orphan was getting irritable with the line of questioning, probably because he was hungry. "I'm from up north, headed south." He wanted to change the subject. "What do you do?" the boy asked.

"I'm a physician," he answered. "Just traveling a ways to visit family."

The boy suddenly cheered up. "Maybe you can help me! I'm seeking treatment for this mark on my face," he blurted, promptly regretting his comment.

"I'm a cardiologist, specializing in treating conditions of the heart. That's unfortunately out of my area of expertise, so I don't think I can help you."

With that, the boy's good cheer receded as quickly as it appeared. "That's okay," he said softly. "I'm traveling to a place that can help." He wanted so badly to believe with all his heart that where he was going could help, but he still had doubts.

"I hope you find what you're looking for. It's interesting: we have but one body, and yet a throng of different types of doctors, each specializing in one specific field. We have a wealth of knowledge about the human body, and still so much that remains unknown."

"What about you?" the orphan asked. "Do you know all there is to know about the human heart?"

"Oh, how I wish that I did. I can help restore a person's health only so much."

"Who then is able?" the boy inquired while sitting up straight.

"I'll tell you, I do know the design and complexities of the human body are too extraordinary to have developed by chance." The doctor sipped his coffee and resumed his train of thought. "Take blood, for example. There is so much going on within the blood. You have plasma, the liquid element of blood. Then platelets promote clotting and help control bleeding when there's a wound. Red blood cells move oxygen from the lungs throughout the body, and then transfers carbon dioxide back to the lungs as waste...quite efficient really. Then there are white blood cells which fight off infection. It's all pretty remarkable when you think about it. And blood channels nourishment, hormones, and antibodies wherever there's a need in the body."

The good doctor was interrupted by the waiter delivering their food. The orphan tore into his cheeseburger without hesitation. It seemed as if he had not eaten in days.

"Slow down there. That burger's not going anywhere!" The doctor took a modest bite of his turkey sandwich before continuing. "Anyway, there is life in the blood. Have you ever heard of the Law of Biogenesis?"

The boy shook his head back and forth with rounded cheeks packed with food. The doctor removed his glasses and smiled. "It basically says that life always comes from life. There are no exceptions. A man named Louis Pasteur, way back in the mid-1800s, solidified this law with his own experiments. It's now a trusted theory—life comes from life.

"There are so many other intricacies." The man picked up the half of sandwich he had started eating and looked at it. "Take this sandwich. It's pleasing to the sight. My stomach tells me I'm hungry, and my mouth begins to water when I contemplate it." Bringing it near his mouth he continued, "By chance, my nose is directly above my mouth, so when I take a bite, I smell the wonderful aroma." He takes a bite. "Now, again by chance, I can taste the diverse flavors of this sandwich: the bread, the turkey, the cheese, lettuce and tomato, and the dressing. I mean, what are the odds that I would have taste buds all over my tongue for such pleasure? And the saliva from my mouth watering has already begun digesting the food to send into the blood stream. As I bite this pickle spear, my ears hear the crisp crunch of the snap."

The boy was listening, but not yet impressed. He grabbed a couple of his fries and dipped them in ketchup. "What are you getting at?" he asked impatiently.

"That all my senses have come to life! We eat for survival, naturally, and yet we receive enormous enjoyment in doing so.

Three times a day, or more!" The man observed the boy for a reaction. "How is this possible, unless we were created by an intelligent Being?" The orphan slurped his drink with little emotion.

"And we haven't even discussed the digestive system and all that goes on there." The physician held out his hands and began counting his fingers as he spoke. "Or the nervous system, the lymphatic system, circulatory system, endocrine system, respiratory system, reproductive system, the wonders of childbirth, or the miracle of healing. The body fights infection and heals itself without any thought of our own—it's ludicrous if you think about it!

"How did the liver develop, to cleanse the body of toxins?" the man asked. "And what about the lungs taking in air, the heart pumping on its own accord, sweat glands to cool the body, and eyebrows to hinder the sweat from blurring the eyes?"

Now wide-eyed for dramatic effect, the boy dropped his burger on his plate and stared at the man as if he had gone a bit mad in his brief rant.

"Think about the eyeball for a minute," the doctor resumed unruffled by the lad's theatrics. "How does it detect such a spectrum of colors, a clarity of surroundings, with eyelids that blink spontaneously to keep them functioning properly? And we haven't even begun to talk about animals, birds, fish, or anything in nature for that matter!" The orphan plopped his face into his burger and remained motionless for his grand finale.

"If I'm not careful, I fear that I may believe in God before I finish this sandwich!" the doctor quipped and threw his napkin on the table to join the boy's act. The orphan glanced up and laughed aloud.

The two teenage boys ambled down the aisle of the dining car toward them. "Well, look who it is, the circus freak!" the larger boy sneered. Stopping at their table, he pushed the orphan's shoulder sharply. "Didn't they tell you? You're not allowed to eat with the other passengers." The gentle clanging of silverware and conversation in the car all but halted.

The doctor calmly stood up from his seat and confronted the teenagers. "We're trying to enjoy our meal, if you guys don't mind." The bulkier boy shoved the man forcefully and he tumbled into a seat across the aisle. The teenagers burst into laughter, "Stay out of it, old man. Mind your own business."

The man regained his composure, stood back up, and straightened his shirt. And then with one lightening swing of his arm, he slapped the big boy across the face. The orphan stared in disbelief. It was the slap heard round the world…well, at least around the rail car. The teenager's face spun backward in a flash. The large boy reared back with clenched fist, ready to swing in return, but something hindered him. Like an invisible wall or as if time were suspended for a few moments, the bully lingered speechless with arm frozen in mid-air.

The orphan observed an immense hand-shaped welt across the bully's face, on the same side as his own birthmark. He wondered if it was karma that had just taken place, or rather an influence of God—if there is a God. Or simply coincidence. As the teenagers retreated to another railcar, numerous diners

THE ORPHAN DREAMER

erupted in applause. Justice was swiftly served, and a wrong made right. It seems there are people on your side when at times it seems not so, the orphan supposed; nonetheless, most choose to dwell in safety, preferring that others carry out the confronting.

The doctor rejoined the boy at the dining table, and the subtle scraping of silverware resumed.

"Sometimes a person needs a good wake-up call in life," the doctor said, and then devoured a drink of water. "That was a minor one. Hopefully he learns from the small lessons, before a sizable one strikes."

"Thanks for standing up for me; no one's ever done that."

"Well, I will never punch a child, I give you my word," the man replied and picked up his pickle wedge again. He took a melodramatic bite creating a loud snap. "But I will *slap* one."

The physician placed his glasses back on with a sophisticated charm. "Now, what were we even talking about?"

The boy wiped his mouth, now stuffed with fries. "You were talking about blood and guts and stuff," he mumbled, in between chews.

"Ah, yes, enough of that already." The cardiologist watched the boy bite into his burger and noticed burger juice dribbling down his chin. "Health is a valuable treasure, don't ever forget. People need a healthy heart. It's the core, the very essence of an individual; beyond that, you have nothing really.

"Surprisingly, some don't know anything about the state of their heart until they finally examine it. By that point, you may reveal a serious problem in need of dire repair. Perhaps an issue is polluting the heart necessitating surgery to rid the problem. Oftentimes, the matter is so deeply rooted within the heart that it takes a nearly impossible revision to restore it."

The boy was casually circling a french fry in his ketchup. He was thoroughly confused on whether the man was speaking about the heart as a blood-pumping organ or as a person's soul. He felt within himself something tugging, as if he needed to be renewed in some manner.

"Every now and then," the doctor continued, "I am privileged to implant in someone a new heart, a completely different heart than the one they've always known. I'm able to offer them a revived life. They walk away with a fresh outlook, with a wholly different mindset."

Still unclear on the doctor's insight, the orphan asked, "How do you know so much about people?"

"Maybe it comes with the job. I help my patients the best that I can, but plenty is out of my control. I hear rumors of a great Physician who can mend a life more notably than I, though," he confessed while grabbing his sandwich. "But that's hearsay. I'm still not sold on the idea."

SIX

Back in his seat, the orphan enjoyed a lengthy nap with a satisfied stomach. The District of Columbia came and went while visions during his early morning slumber burst to life once more. An elation swept over the lad as he splashed through a celestially lucid lagoon. Charcoal smoke zigzagged high in the air from ancient Spanish ships ablaze below.

"Excuse me." The boy stirred from his sleep and opened his eyes. "Excuse me, sir," a young train attendant repeated herself to a man sitting just behind the boy. "Smoking is no longer allowed on any of the train cars. I'm sorry, but you'll have to put that out." Smoke hung heavily in the air and the orphan rubbed his eyes, now stinging from the fumes.

Peering out the train window, the boy was lured into the dense darkness. Obscure trees rushed by as neurotic phantoms, visible only by the dim lights of the train. He was unable to see past the tree line skirting the cars, only dark recesses whispering of countless unknowns beyond. He remembered that he had only enough money remaining for food and his current ticket to Atlanta. Once there, he would have no choice but to depart the train and find his own way.

He couldn't believe he was out on his own, and pondered his decision in running away from the convent. Staring out the window as nearby terrain flashed past, it reminded him of life, steadily moving forward and pausing for no one. He envisioned throwing an object from the train. He would never get it back. Just like making a poor choice in life, one may never retrieve it, but must suffer the consequences of the poor decision. There is always a repercussion, whether a noble or bad choice is made. Negative consequences, he determined, must serve to refine behavior. If only a person would recognize the cause and effect of choice and reaction, he might choose more wisely in the future.

The ride to Atlanta was a long one, and wishing to stretch his legs, the orphan decided to take a stroll. Along the way, a few people were reading, some sleeping, and others chatting or playing a game. Two cars behind his, a gracefully weathered lady was alone and sound asleep. He wished he had brought something to read for the trip as he noticed a few books loosely piled on the seat beside the woman. Continuing on to the next rail car, the boy had a brilliant idea. He spun around and began walking back nonchalantly.

THE ORPHAN DREAMER

Upon reaching the napping woman again, he calmly paused and thumbed through the short stack of books next to her. One caught his eye, *The Mirror Divide*, and he casually gathered it to his side and drifted back to his seat two cars ahead with a sense of pride. Nobody suspected he had lifted the book, and now he could pass the time with one of his favorite pastimes—reading. He felt bad for taking it, his heart told him it was wrong. But he had so little, and owned no books of his own. She had several, and undoubtedly many more at home!

The orphan read for a couple of hours, and the more he read, the further engrossed he became. It compared life to a one-way mirror, the glass dividing humanity between the living and the deceased. Those who pass through the mirror depart into the next life. But none are permitted to return to warn the remain of what lies upon the other side. Only God is able to monitor each side of the mirrored divide, while those living in the flesh observe only the mirrored reflection of their own present life. It spoke of a God who began the world, who promised to return, and who even bisected history itself with the division of B.C. and A.D.

The book went on to reveal the meaning of life and an individual's unique calling on this current side of the mirror. We each possess one life to weather, it explained, one brief sojourn upon earth before transferring to an adjacent dimension. It urged the pursuit of fulfilling the specific purpose and mission of one's existence: *to glorify God and live according to his ways.*

He shut the book with a thud and set it down beside him, suddenly feeling guilty again for swiping the book in the first place. The philosophy proved a rather compelling viewpoint until the part about glorifying God. He wished that he had

31

snatched one of the other books instead. Perhaps the others would have proven more inspirational.

⌒

The screeching brakes of the train awoke the boy from a peaceful nap. An anxious murmuring filled the cabin as passengers pressed against the windows for a better view outside. A crew member waltzed through each rail car explaining the minor predicament. The conductor had received an alert of a tree that had fallen across the tracks up ahead. Help was on the way to have it removed, and they would be on their way as soon as possible. Nothing to worry, and if anyone wanted to get off the train to walk around for a few minutes, they were welcome to do so. He affirmed the train would be on its way again within an hour.

While most passengers remained on board, the orphan led the way outside into the mid-morning sun. People talked, introduced themselves, and squinted to witness the enormous tree being surgically removed. The rumble of chain saws reverberated down the tracks and echoed through the hollow clearing for the passage of the train. It was not long before all passengers were directed back onto the train to resume their journey down the track.

Back in his seat, the boy grew bored once again. He whipped his head around and glanced at the adjoining seat. His eyes sprung open—the book—it was gone! He searched beneath the seats and inside and around his backpack. With all the commotion of the emergency train stop and going outside, he forgot to hide the book in his backpack! But where was it? Someone certainly took it. His temples tightened as he started

THE ORPHAN DREAMER

to get angry, and then the irony hit him, as he remembered that it was he who stole it first.

But that was different, he defended himself, for he had been unfairly treated his entire life—he was owed! And besides, others had an unfair advantage that he lacked, for he had no parents, no money, and was alone. He was bullied and teased and few showed concern.

He looked out the window and observed a herd of cattle grazing upon a grassy field. They possessed nothing, and yet, appeared content. Surely they didn't feel sorry for themselves, he supposed. His temples relaxed and he slumped in his seat. Anyone can justify what they do, he decided. Regardless of how immoral the action, every individual is right in his or her mind and is justified in the behavior. Even the privileged person believes he is entitled to anything he wants and whenever he wants it, and assumes the victim when denied.

Just then, a railcar door opened and the orphan observed a familiar weathered lady wandering down the aisle toward him. It was the book lady! From a distance, he could barely make out the title of the book she carried: *The Mirror Divide.* Without thinking, he instinctively looked away in the other direction. He started to sweat and his hands began to tremble. As she neared, he grew agitated at the woman, as if she committed the shameful deed of theft herself.

While she stopped to chat with another woman, he concluded that he certainly must have a conscience to determine right from wrong. But how, especially if we came from nothing—unless some manner of moral code was written upon our hearts? Animals didn't seem to have the same capacity for conviction that he endured. Amongst other things, this no doubt separates man from animal.

33

What a mystery, the conscience of humanity, the boy further considered. The tree obstructing the tracks could have proven disastrous had the conductor not listened to the forewarning he received. Who knows the damage and injury that would have resulted had the conductor neglected the caution? The conscience forewarns of potential harm and encourages a change in behavior before it's too late. Obstacles will inevitably occur in life, he thought, some small, some not so small, and we must be careful to heed the warnings of the soul.

The lady patted her new friend on the shoulder and proceeded down the aisle toward the boy. "Pardon me," she began. The orphan turned to face his adversary, ready to justify his role in the heist. "Good day," she said. "If I'm not mistaken, I do believe you were reading this book earlier. I took it back while you were away, and honestly, I felt entitled and pleased in doing so. But I have since felt sorry for my response and would rather you read it than not. If you could only return it when you are done, I would appreciate it." And with that, she extended to him the book. He said not a word, but accepted it out of courtesy, even though he had no intention of reading it anymore.

The woman gave the boy a peaceful wink and walked back to her rail car. To his shock, the orphan fought back a tear. He felt ashamed and unworthy of her kindness. How could a person show such compassion toward another upon being cheated? That's not normal. Her reaction was attractive and he could not stop thinking about it. He wanted that unexpected and uncommon quality in himself, that others might be drawn to him as he felt toward the woman...not in a physical way, but emotional. He must alter his perspective, he insisted, to let go of his bitterness, to forgive when others offend him, and to press on. He knew it wouldn't be easy, but he had to try.

SEVEN

The dining car was bustling with hungry patrons. Sitting alone, the lad welcomed the solitude at his table. He ate his club sandwich and bowl of diced fruit meaningfully, still contemplating the book lady's kindness toward him. This was the last real meal he could afford, with only a couple of dollars remaining afterward. The journey ahead was yet a long one, but he was grateful for how far the money had carried him. He was on a mission, unsure exactly where it might lead him, but he would make it somehow. He would figure things out along the way, and if he ended up starving, he would accept his lot. Fate was in control now, come good or bad. His course was set and he would embrace the outcome.

After eating, he returned to his rail car and noticed an influx of passengers. The train stop, while he ate in the dining room, clearly ushered in a company of new travelers. A mother cautiously eyed the orphan from two rows ahead as he made his way through the car. As he passed by, she casually swung her arm like a seatbelt across her child's torso seated beside her and held her gaze upon the intruder. The orphan knew it was in light of his alarming birthmark and didn't hold it against her. As bothersome as it was, she was protecting her kid instinctively, as a mama bear her cub.

A suited man with tie was already settled into the seat next to his, and the boy slithered past him to claim his own. "How do you do?" the suited man asked.

"Fine, I suppose," the boy replied as he plopped into his seat. "How are you?"

"How am I, you ask? That's a complex question." The man fidgeted and looked at his watch. "I travel all the time, and these trips are exhausting. I used to love traveling—*loved* it— but not anymore. It's draining...not as enjoyable as people think after a while. People everywhere, the noise, pollution, delays." The man paused and then snickered to himself. "Financially speaking, I'm doing outstanding—no complaints! Well, that's not entirely true, there are some complaints." He reached into his suit jacket and pulled out a miniature, single-serve bottle of whiskey. "Care for a swig?" he asked, extending the bottle toward the boy.

"No, thanks. What complaints do you have?"

"Where do I begin? There are constant threats when one earns an abundance of money. People are forever after your wealth, after your possessions...even after your time. Heaven forbid you have free time! Not to mention a measure of anxiety and insomnia. How I would cherish a full night's sleep!"

"Is that all?" the boy questioned. The puzzled man furrowed his brow sternly. "What do you mean, is that all?"

"It sounds like you're upset because you're making a lot of money. And your problems are brought about as a result of your success."

"Well, if you must know, it's the wife—ex-wife, I mean," the wealthy man corrected himself. He unscrewed the whiskey cap, held the tiny bottle to his mouth, and threw it back with a sudden fling of his head. "She divorced me. I could never make her happy."

"Why'd she leave?" the boy pressed the man.

"Good question. I gave her everything she ever wanted: a huge home, nice cars, vacations, you name it. Meanwhile, I'm always traveling for business, very stressful at times. She says I cheated on her; she blames *me* for the divorce." There was an awkward pause as the suited man pulled another minibar bottle from his coat, removed the lid, and flung it back as fast as the first.

"Well?" the boy inquired.

"Well what?" the man challenged defensively with a drawn-out sigh.

"Did you cheat?"

"You wouldn't understand, kid; it's not how you think. Life is demanding, it's complicated. I just need to release some steam now and then. I'm human, for crying out loud. The girls never meant anything to me. I always returned to my wife, I would never leave her." He searched the boy's face for empathy. "She doesn't understand. She never works. But I've always been committed to my wife. Now she's taken half of my wealth, both kids, and I've had to sell properties in order to compensate her. Don't get me wrong, I'm still a rich man. I just hate to see her getting what she doesn't deserve."

The orphan was silent, as bitterness toward the man welled up inside. He was a self-centered man, and his kids suffered because of him. Now they had no father, simply because he lacked commitment and would not sacrifice for the sake of his wife and children. He justified his affairs and made himself the victim of his own wrongdoing. Interestingly, the man actually believed that *he* was the victim. The boy perceived that it must get easier to justify an immoral behavior the more it is committed, as if the conscience grew numb each time it was ignored.

"At least you had a choice," the orphan blurted. "You didn't have to lose your kids. Neither of my parents wanted me, so they sent me to a convent where I was abused and treated like dirt." He regretted saying anything, but the words were unyielding.

Now the businessman was offended. "Stop blaming others!" he rebuked the lad. "Be a man! Take responsibility for your own life. You're accountable for your days."

"You're a hypocrite!" the orphan exclaimed as he stood up to leave. Withdrawing swiftly, he found an empty seat in the next rail car. He breathed deeply and calmed down while pondering their argument. He couldn't forgive this man, he thought. No way, and he couldn't forgive his own parents for their selfishness. And neither could he forgive the convent nor the other orphans for their abuse. How can some forgive and others cannot. It made no sense. If someone hurts you, you can't just let it go and dismiss it—it's impossible.

He considered the rich man. He had everything it seemed: money, possessions, confidence. And yet, it brought him a host of problems: an air of entitlement, a shallow existence, a feeling of entrapment. Making money is time-consuming and one is never wealthy enough. Money will never solve your real problems, the boy realized. He heard once that the world is not driven by greed, as often believed, but by envy. Everyone is envious of others and the fact that they have more than they. He recalled what the wise blind woman had said: that joy is indeed a choice. Whether a person is wealthy or poor, it matters not—one can be thankful and joyful just the same.

A train attendant paused at his row and offered complimentary snacks to the passengers. She reached over with a basket full of bagged chips, pretzels, and nuts. "They're free?" the boy asked, a bit shocked. "Yes, feel free to take what you like," she replied with a motherly smile.

Grabbing two handfuls indiscriminately, he jammed the goodies into his backpack. "Oh my!" the attendant blurted and laughed. A plump woman sitting next to the boy took a bag of pretzels and placed it in her lap. Before the attendant could escape down the aisle, the orphan seized two more bags and said thank you.

As the attendant made her way, the portly lady explained to her new companion her rule of *everything in moderation.* "In everything a balance, in everything its rightful place," she began pretentiously. "Tattered attire is neither fitting nor proper, and yet expensive clothing is outright vanity. When at a gathering, enjoy a drink if you fancy, for it is polite," she continued, "but never two; there is no excuse in having two and no shame in the things you might do."

She patted the boy on the knee. "Now listen closely and this one shall serve you well. No need to starve yourself, but eat not

AARON BROWN

to boredom or your clothes will surely tell." The boy glimpsed at the well-fed woman's body without her notice and rolled his eyes. "Even if it is free," she droned on, "it's not worth it. Besides, the pleasure of eating dwindles the more an item is consumed, until a person is merely indulging for the sake of something to do and passing the time of day."

And with that, the orphan balled up his jacket against the window and burrowed his head within it. After a fruitful rest, the train was minutes from arriving in Atlanta. He examined his map to see how much further he had to travel to reach Mexico. It was still far away and he had two dollars to his name. He politely returned his borrowed book to the book lady and departed the train.

EIGHT

Burly, ominous clouds rolled in with a surge of wind. The orphan scoured the streets intentionally, looking for some means of shelter before the storm's assault. Traffic was light with the onset of evening. Lightening threatened and rain began to softly sprinkle. Only a few blocks from the train station, warm lights from an old church glowed through stained glass windows. The rain picked up, so the boy bolted to the front porch of the church for cover. He would wait out the rain between the columns of the portico, he decided, and then move on.

Two old-fashioned sconce lights dimly lit the porch. Thankful for the snacks he had grabbed on the train, he removed a bag of nuts from his backpack. Tearing it open, he took a bite and noticed a single moth buzzing from sconce to sconce. With the rain confining the moth within the bounds of the patio, it seemed satisfied flying to and fro while smacking into the glass fixtures. Squinting, the boy observed several dead moths inside each sconce. What struck the boy as odd was that each fixture was entirely open and exposed at the top. That meant the moths could have freely flown away from the light to safety, but they instead chose to linger in the heat and die.

Halfway through the bag, one of the front doors opened and an enthusiastic gentleman invited the boy inside. The preacher, at the other end of the sanctuary, nodded his head at the newcomer with a distant, yet personal welcome. Sitting near the rear of the chapel, the lad resumed his snack, munching as quietly as possible. It was an evening service, and few congregants in the half-full room even noticed his arrival. He couldn't explain it, but the boy felt an overwhelming sense of security. An unspeakable aura of feeling at home permeated the room.

"So there were ten men with leprosy, and they stood aways off and pleaded with Jesus for mercy," the preacher proceeded to the assembly. "Jesus gave them a simple directive, almost too simple to accept, if you think about it: Show yourselves to the priests. That was it! Since leprosy is contagious, lepers had to remain isolated from other people. And if a leper ever believed himself healed, he needed a priest to declare him clean before he could gather again with others. So while they were still disfigured with skin scabbing, sores, and lumps, Jesus instructed them to go and show the priests that they were no longer infected. Doesn't seem rational, if you ask me."

The pastor scanned his audience deliberately to sharpen his point. "But they obeyed, and on their way to the priests, they were healed. It took an act of faith on their part." He paused a brief moment before continuing. "Now one of them returned and fell on his face before Jesus and gave thanks. 'Where are the

THE ORPHAN DREAMER

other nine?' Jesus asked. 'Has only one returned to praise God?'"

The orphan was shocked that only one man returned to give thanks. Most people ask for help, he noticed, but do they give praise when it comes? Or do they justify that the help would have come anyway had they not asked?

"And then Jesus affirmed that it was the man's faith, his *faith*, that made him well!" the preacher passionately exclaimed.

The minister had the orphan's full attention. He had to have faith in order to be restored, he considered. He remembered being taught long ago that it was impossible to please God *without* faith. But how could he discover healing if he wasn't even sure that God existed? Nobody can prove there is a God, and he supposed, neither can anyone prove otherwise. What if God was waiting for a person to step out and believe with the limited knowledge and insight he possessed? On the other hand, maybe the healing pool was sufficient without a belief in God. One thing was certain, though: a person must have some level of faith, or nothing would happen. He must take action and assume some risk. Only then could a person grow and be shaped and realize change within himself.

"Another time," the preacher launched into an additional narrative, "there was a commander of an army named Naaman, who also suffered from leprosy. A prophet, a man of God named Elisha, instructed Naaman that if he would go and wash himself seven times in the Jordan River, he would be restored and clean. This upset Naaman, for he thought Elisha was going to call on God and miraculously wave his hand over his leprosy. And besides that, there were other rivers nearby more esteemed and cleaner than the Jordan. So he left angry."

The story reminded the boy of the healing pool. What are the odds that he would stumble into a church relaying this

43

account? Was it confirmation for his dream? It's probably just because his dream is prevalent in his mind, nothing more. Like when you search for yellow cars and you suddenly begin noticing yellow cars like never before.

"Now Naaman's servants," the preacher continued, "reasoned that had the prophet told him to do something extraordinary, he would have done it. How much more so should he obey in such an easy task, to dip in the Jordan and be cleansed. So Naaman listened and went down and dunked himself in the Jordan seven times, and his skin was renewed and became like the skin of a young child."

The orphan was again inspired. Naaman believed, took action, and received healing. He will do the same: he believes in the power of the healing pool, he has responded in traveling there, and will one day arrive at his destination and receive restoration. The preacher promptly looked directly at the boy with unmistakeable tenderness in his voice. "Most people are physically flawed in some manner, as was the leper, but make no mistake and hear me well—all are flawed *internally*. Every one of us. One must bow at the foot of the cross. Humbly, lowly, and with repentance, each must surrender to Christ. The treasure of life is discovered at the foot of the cross—nowhere else."

A handful of people climbed on stage as the minister took a seat in the front row. They each grabbed an instrument and began playing as the lyrics to a modern song flashed on a big screen. There were hymnals, no organ like he was used to, and the audience was acting like they were enjoying themselves and actually wanting to sing. Everyone stood, some gently swayed to the rhythm, and a couple lifted their arms with palms extended in worship. One elderly woman even clapped to the beat of the drums. This was all foreign, the orphan reflected, as these

THE ORPHAN DREAMER

people seemed to genuinely feel intently, to believe what they sang, almost as if they were truly singing to some Being who was listening. It was simultaneously strange and alluring.

The storm strengthened as everyone dispersed, sprinting to their cars. The orphan waited for the crowd to scatter, hoping the rain would ease up for his stroll through town. A firm hand caught him on the shoulder from behind and he swung around to recognize the face of the pastor attached to the intrusive grip. "And with whom might I have the pleasure of meeting?" asked the minister. The boy introduced himself and admitted that he simply ducked in to weather the storm. A heartfelt smile flooded the man's face as he shook the lad's hand.

NINE

It was the most comfortable bed he had ever slept in: soft sheets, fluffy comforter, cloud-like pillow, and a room all to himself. By the time he awoke, the sun was well into the sky. The scent of homemade waffles and crispy bacon lured him downstairs where he was greeted by the preacher and his wife. "Good morning, young man!" the wife embraced the lad with a warmhearted hug. "How'd you sleep?"

"I've never slept that well—or that long before." The boy sat at the kitchen table where they had a place all set for him. "I hope you're hungry!" said the husband while pouring a glass of orange juice for the guest.

"Thank you both for inviting me into your home like this. Don't worry, I won't stay long. I don't want to be in the way."

"Don't be silly. Both of our kids are grown and gone; we have two spare bedrooms collecting dust. And whatever you find in the fridge or pantry, help yourself—don't be shy." The man opened the refrigerator to reveal a jammed fridge full of an assortment of food. "My wife loves to entertain guests more than anything in the world: be it dinners, game nights, or parties. She's always dreamed of having a second refrigerator entirely for drinks. We have the perfect spot for another one in the garage. Some day I'll surprise her with one."

"You've promised me another fridge for years!" his wife teased. "One day," she mimicked. Turning to the boy, she insisted, "You are more than welcome to stay until you figure things out."

It was a deal. It was like having actual parents. Now there were rules, and some similar to those at the convent, but he was living in a real home for the first time! There were chores around the house he must complete, and he would be required to attend church while living under their roof. He was also expected to work, at least part time, and could keep and save all the money he earned. "There are plenty of jobs to do around the church, if you'd like," the pastor offered. "For pay, of course."

"That sounds wonderful. I can start right away!"

At night, the church building looked fairly decent, but daylight was less merciful, revealing considerable neglect. A member of the church helped the boy realign the hinges on the front doors, as they hung a bit crooked—not terribly, but noticeable to the keen eye. They sanded both rustic doors and painted them a bright jade. The majestic color popped amidst the surrounding pearl white brick. Several people strolling along the front sidewalk complimented the workers, encouraging them to find other ways to enhance the property. Throughout the week, they spruced up the yard, pulled weeds, trimmed hedges, and designed new flower beds. Hard-to-reach light bulbs were changed high up around the roof awning and church tower.

The preacher emerged as the orphan was admiring their handiwork of the property grounds. "We're all finished!" the boy proclaimed, well pleased.

"It looks absolutely stunning!" the minister replied, surveying the area like one might a painting. "But finished?" He met the lad's eyes and watched his enthusiasm recede. "What about the interior of the church?"

"The interior?" the boy gasped. The idea never occurred to him.

"Well, of course!" the man smiled and held a broad bag up in the air. "Come have lunch with me," he added. The pastor led the lad to a garden bed blanketed in fresh bark mulch, with a newly added concrete bench in the center. After sitting, the man emptied the bag and arranged fried chicken, mac and cheese, collard greens, and buttermilk biscuits on the bench in between them.

"I love what you've done out here," he continued. "But the building needs a good deal of restoration and remodeling on the inside as well. It reminds me of a story in the Bible."

Rolling his eyes, the boy asked sarcastically, "Does everything remind you of the Bible?"

The pastor laughed aloud. "That's funny! I suppose a lot does remind me of it." After a bite, he looked at the church and began, "Jesus was talking to a group of religious leaders back in the day. He called them blind guides, fools, and hypocrites—he

THE ORPHAN DREAMER

has a way of making friends," he joked. "He accused them of preaching, but not practicing what they preached, and that they do good deeds only to be seen by others." He pointed to his own church. "There are many here who do the same. They appear noble to people around them. But Jesus sees them differently; he looks at the heart."

"This is the best fried chicken I've ever had—and biscuits," interrupted the boy. "But what is that?" He pointed and held his eyes open as wide as he could.

"Those are collard greens! They're famous down here...try some."

"No thanks! Those are yours. I'll have more mac and cheese, though."

"So anyway," the man persisted. "Jesus went on to explain to the religious leaders that they clean the outside of a cup and plate, but not the inside. He said they were like white-washed tombs, which appear lovely outwardly, but were full of dead people's bones and filth within. In other words, they seemed righteous to others, but they were actually hypocritical and corrupt."

"Are you going to eat that last biscuit?" the orphan asked.

"No, it's all yours. Hard to find biscuits that good." The man grabbed a crispy chicken thigh. "It's kind of like this chicken. The outside is golden brown, crunchy, and delicious, but if the chicken itself were rotten, the entire piece is bad... and unsafe. Does that make sense?"

The boy chewed rapidly and swallowed. "Yes, I believe so."

"Good. It's all about the heart. The outside facade of a person is not as critical. When a person surrenders his heart to God, he loses his self. And in losing his self, it is then that a person *finds* himself."

"I think I get it," the boy said with uncertainty.

49

"All right then. Well anyway, it's sort of like this chapel here," the man said with a grin and wiped his mouth of fried chicken grease. "It needs to be cleaned within. We need to paint the main room, reseal the concrete floor, clean the windows, reorganize the library, and rearrange the Sunday school room. There's much work to be done!"

The following Sunday, the chapel floors gleamed and everyone complimented the sage green interior walls. The orphan attended the service as he agreed, and he chose a seat near the center of the room, with people sitting all around him. And though he did not agree with everything the pastor believed, he respected him and listened attentively.

"We each possess a special calling in life to do extraordinary things," began the minister. "When we walk with God, he plants desires in us that align with his purposes. If we turn to him and align our moral compass with his, God will bless our efforts and fuel our endeavors. He will lead and inspire his followers to fulfill their personal calling when they seek his will above their own. That's humility, a yielded obedience wanting God's will to be done. These will realize true fulfillment in life, and God will use both the positive and negative circumstances in life for good. He is fully able, for he is fully sovereign."

The boy couldn't help but feel a personal calling in his soul to find the healing pool somewhere in Mexico. Maybe there was more to it than he imagined. Perhaps there was a higher purpose that he had yet to understand.

"But the remaining who desire their will above God's," the minister continued, "will find themselves forever grasping at the wind, curiously unable to find fulfillment. They toil in opposition to God, never able to secure their hopes and dreams. Setting out on a personal mission apart from God is dangerous. The path is cloudy and confusing, while the umbrella of God's protection evades us. We venture alone, with pitfalls and setbacks and unrest. Joy and satisfaction forever elude us, and the years sail by engulfed in regret."

Immediately following the service, the preacher retired to his church office to pray, which was his custom. In the dimly lit room, he knelt with knees resting upon a pillow, and his upper body hunched over a sofa. With eyes open, he gazed upward and pleaded with God, "Father, open the ears of some here tonight, give them a hunger and thirst for you. May you enlighten them, bless them with conviction and lowliness of soul, and speak to them. I pray the words they heard this evening would resonate and cut to their core. May they be desperate for you, empty apart from you, and may you grant them restlessness until they find rest in you. Awaken them, Father, that they might no longer compromise, but turn wholeheartedly to you."

A few days later, the minister's wife surprised the lad with some new clothes and a new pair of shoes she thought he would enjoy. Never had he been treated with such kindness. She washed his clothing, cooked meals, and her husband continually introduced him to friends and taught him new ideas and ways of doing things.

"Why have neither of you asked about my parents?" the boy finally asked the man. And not once had either of them ever brought up his horrid birthmark, he reflected, as if neither had even noticed.

"Why don't we go for a walk?" the preacher suggested. The two of them slipped out the front door and headed down the road. "We're not here to judge or to cast blame, regardless of your situation or anyone's situation. We simply want to help people, to offer direction."

"I appreciate all you both have done for me. Soon I'll be on my way to complete my journey. I know it's my destiny to follow the path I am on."

The pastor looked concerned. "Just be sure you are following God's lead. We have free will to choose our future, but without God, we go alone and without his blessing." They reached a four-way intersection and the man pointed toward three different routes they could take. "Free will leads to multiple paths, some good, some destructive, all depending upon the heart. Having freedom to choose is indeed a blessing but will prove a curse if contrary to the ways of God."

The boy had heard all of that before. "But I've tried praying numerous times to know the will of God. He does not hear, nor does he answer."

"Well, you have to be connected. If you try to call someone without phone service, your call will not go through. In the same way, prayer to God fails when you are not connected with him. You must surrender your life, your will, to Christ. He died for you. But if you're still carrying the burden of your sins, you're still condemned, and you won't be able to get through. The line is disconnected."

The lad was beginning to regret the walk. He was growing in understanding, but still not willing to commit. "I hear what you're saying, but I'm just not ready. I'm young and have my whole life ahead of me."

"Don't wait too long. Promise me you won't die before you decide to follow Christ."

The boy felt depressed. "I can't promise you that."

The preacher gave the boy a gentle nudge. "I know you can't." The return home was a quiet one.

Sunday morning arrived and the windows never sparkled like they did that day. Sunlight radiated through the beveled glass panes and danced upon the bustling crowd. The church library was cleaned and polished, and all books were more appropriately organized according to topic. An efficient system in locating books was established and an orderly filing practice set in place. And finally, the Sunday school room was rearranged to accommodate a comfortable ambience with improved lighting and acoustics. The orphan had worked hard all week and was proud of his accomplishments.

The minister thanked the boy and others who had helped in the renovations, and then he plunged right into the morning sermon. He was notably different today. "I have preached in this chapel for many years now. I look out and see friends whom I have known for a long, long time." Beads of sweat formed on his forehead, and his voice grew passionate and personal. "I love you all, and I say this from my affection for you. A number of you believe that you know the Lord, when in fact you do not. And neither does he know some of you. You are deceived."

The entire assembly was still and hushed. Everyone listened intently amidst an extended pause. The preacher wiped his forehead. "Many do not perceive their need for a Savior, nor do they fathom any sense of urgency in the matter." He spoke theatrically, yet with genuineness and singularity of purpose. "I implore you to turn to God tonight. Do it now! Do not wait, lest you brood over your decision and die on the way home." Several people now squirmed and fidgeted in their seats; all were on edge.

"This chapel has never been this clean. And yet your hearts are polluted and defiled. So many of you deceive yourselves by playing church. You profess to believe, but your actions prove otherwise. I urge you to break up your fallow ground and renew your hearts. You must bow at the foot of the cross and place your trust in Jesus. There your treasure lies, at the foot of the cross," he again affirmed.

And with that, as if pressed for time, he rushed off the stage and vanished down the hallway and into his study. It was, by far, his shortest sermon ever. The band leapt onto the stage, two songs were sung, and then all were solemnly dismissed.

The preacher grieved over the lost souls in his congregation and poured his heart out to God in great agony, such angst he suffered for his people that his heart felt no more, and with that, it beat its last.

A few minutes following, the orphan went to the church study to check on the man of God. After knocking softly, he cracked open the door and called his name. With no reply, he

THE ORPHAN DREAMER

stepped in and scanned the dimly lit office. In the center of the room, he saw the preacher kneeling upon a pillow with his body slumped over the sofa. By the abnormal contour of his body and the dreadful look on his face, the boy knew it was pointless in calling his name again.

⟋

The following morning, a grown son and daughter arrived at the preacher's house to comfort their mother. They hugged and cried at length. The daughter noticed the orphan in the next room and clearly asked for all to hear, "What is he still doing here?"

"It's okay, dear," her mom replied. "He's totally fine. It's actually been nice having a guest in the house with all of you gone—not so lonesome."

The son swiftly perked up and joined in. "Well, we're here now." He swung around and glanced at the orphan. "When are you leaving, by the way?" he bluntly asked.

"That is enough!" his mother scolded. "Not another word about it."

The orphan realized he was once more the outsider, an outcast within the home that so recently lent him compassion and affection. He would need to get going and resume his calling, perhaps even discovering his purpose in life. He pondered the pastor's passing and reasoned that sometimes good befalls upon the wicked and at other times adversity strikes upon the godly. Life is not always fair, he concluded.

Later that evening, when the adult children stepped out of the house and the mother was alone in the kitchen, the orphan put his arms around her firmly. She embraced him back and

55

held him tighter than she had her own children. Tears gushed from each of them: from the woman, for the heavy loss of her soulmate, and from the lad for so many reasons.

The orphan cried for the death of the man who took him in and cared for him. He grieved for the agony of the man's wife in her time of pain and isolation. He wept for his rejection once again, this time by those close to one so dear to him. He mourned for his need to say goodbye to a couple who had showered such grace and kindness upon him—the only real home he had ever known. But most of all, he sobbed for himself: a self-centered lament and self pity in again being alone, with no friend, without parent, without family, without a God. If only a God did exist, at least he could find comfort that a Being far greater than he had everything under control, was sovereign over the affairs of the world, and who orchestrated them for his perfect purposes.

The boy secretly gathered his belongings in the guest room that night, along with the money he had earned while working for the church. He was grateful for the job and for the home, and decided to keep only a portion of his gain for food.

Three hours later, when all were asleep, the orphan snuck out and disappeared down the street. Three days following, a large truck pulled up in front of the house and an almond-colored refrigerator was delivered into the garage...in just the perfect spot.

TEN

All morning, hiking through the city of Atlanta, the boy pondered the preacher's passion in convincing others of their need for God. How he had yearned for his parishioners to believe and commit their lives to One who died for them that they might live. With such anguish of soul and spirit of prayer for some to repent that his heart could no longer endure. Who holds such confidence in his faith as to forfeit his life for another? Few express the measure of surrender as this preacher had demonstrated, the orphan decided. Scores of churchgoers profess the same, and yet differ in lifestyle as wide as the sea. The majority appear pious on Sunday morning, but regress to indifference the remainder of the week. The preacher was different. His life and death were a testimony of his faith and abandonment to his beliefs.

That afternoon, he enjoyed a leisurely lunch at a deli and rested in a nearby park. A mom and her children played on a swing set, and a dad and his son tossed a frisbee back and forth. The orphan was personally grateful for having had a taste of what a healthy family was like. Having only lived there for several weeks, he considered Atlanta his home, for home should be a place of refuge, a sanctuary of acceptance and affection. One day he would return.

By early evening, he had resumed his journey to the outskirts of town. On two occasions, a car passed him by and slowed to a stop, with the intention of offering the boy a ride. But each time, as the boy approached, the driver would observe his heinous birthmark and speed away. His gaze fixed upon the pavement; he realized most people were uncaring and wished the preacher was still alive. Lifting his head, he stared far into the distance at the road ahead. He looked for some time, almost mesmerized, fantasizing about reaching the healing pool.

By nightfall, the boy had left the city limits far behind. Within a couple of hours, he ascended the top of a roadway hill with pasture land on either side. Resolving to rest for the evening, he hopped over a barbed wire fence and sprawled down in a tranquil, grassy meadow. He was far enough from the street for solitude, but close enough to hear the humming of cars passing through. Lying on his back, he inhaled and exhaled deeply. The countryside had its benefits, he realized, as thousands of stars shimmered playfully overhead in the clear sky. Never would such a vast canopy of lights be visible in the city.

They were so far away, so unfathomably distant and without end. He found comfort in easily spotting Orion—hunter with belt and sword—amidst innumerable stars. Most constellations were unremarkable to him. How could a single star serve a foot, another a hand, and a third depict an eye, and that was supposed to somehow portray an animal? That required too much imagination. But with Orion he could clearly see a clothed man with a belt and sword in an epic battle.

A gentle gust blew across the field and helped him relax. He envisioned himself as the great Hunter on a journey to discover purpose and healing, and with him he wielded a sword of strength and protection. While living in the convent, he had read many books about stars and planets and solar systems. But so much was unknown. How did they come to be, and how are they affixed, so predictably unmoved year after year, suspended in the midst of nothingness? Maybe there does exist an absolute Being and I have been deceived. Perhaps it is not I, the boy considered, but he who is pursuing me. The lad was lured to sleep while contemplating the possible existence of an eternal deity who may have created the world.

A wind blew in from the southern corner of the earth and brought with it the Devil, who advanced upon the young boy in the meadow that evening. The Beast, with thick horns twisting outward and forward from each side of his head, encountered his prey, alone and vulnerable. Throngs of his subjects surrounded the vile creature continually, but most were deceived with no idea of their self-deception. These concerned him not, for they served no threat. But this boy attracted his attention presently. The lad's awareness was heightening, his perception deepening, and light was beginning to permeate the mind of the offensive infidel. The Devil sought to seize the life of the boy and to secure his soul for eternity before it proved too late. Drawing nearer, the great Deceiver bent down and kissed the boy's cheek. The orphan heard voices all around in an unfamiliar dialect.

Suddenly, the boy awoke to the rushing of wind in his hair and a cow licking his face. Other cows were mooing excitedly as if something were agitating them. He jumped up, alarmed and confused, provoking the herd of cows and heifers to scamper away in a frenzy, except for a monstrous lone bull with a massive hump above its shoulders. He stood his ground, staring and snorting at the boy. After stomping his foot on the ground a couple of times, the bull took a step forward.

The boy grabbed his backpack and bolted for the fence, the bull shadowing behind, the distance between them narrowing. The fence was too far to outrun the stampeding bull, so he raced toward a grazing cow along the way. At the last second, he ducked around the innocent cow, completely caught off guard of what was about to transpire. The agitated bull, too late to alter his course, rammed into the cow at full speed, gouging its horns deep within its neck. Both the cow and bull collapsed to the ground beside the boy.

Rising, the lad sprinted once more with bull in high pursuit. Scaling the fence, the boy hooked his pants on a barb, tearing a pant leg and flipping him over the top barbed wire. Slamming down on the other side, his palms bore the brunt of his fall and he rolled onto his back. The bull smashed into the fence, ripping a wooden pole out of the ground and shoving another on its side, barbed wires loosely drooping in between. As the bloody horns wrestled in the tangled wires, the orphan pulled himself up and darted for the road. Barreling across the dangling fence, the bull chased the boy down the middle of the street toward the crest of the hill.

A car surfaced out of nowhere and rounded the top of the ridge. The boy skirted toward the shoulder of the road for safety, but the bull maintained its stride in the street. Lacking sufficient time to react, the driver of the car swerved but smashed into the headstrong bull. Crushing the front end of the car, the bull toppled over the hood and shattered the windshield. The car landed in the ditch beside the road, steam curling upward from the remnants of the engine.

The boy spun around and saw the bull sprawled out in the middle of the road, limbs contorted and mangled, with blood pooling around its lifeless carcass. As he ran to the totaled car, several other vehicles pulled over to help. The driver crawled out, disoriented and bleeding from the top of his head. An ambulance eventually showed up and hauled the motorist away; the fire department did a routine inspection, and a wrecker removed the demolished car.

A crew dragged the bull from the road with much difficulty and left it in the grassy ditch. At last, moaning emanated from the adjacent field, where they noticed a dying cow writhing in pain. A police officer trudged over and examined the animal. Two gun shots exploded and the officer returned with an arrogant strut. Once the officers finally abandoned the area, only the orphan and a state trooper remained at the scene.

"What are your plans from here?" the trooper asked, opening the front door of his squad car.

"I'm just gonna keep walking south," the boy replied. "I'm headed to New Orleans."

"I know it's not much, but I can take you to the Alabama border. Hop in!"

The lad climbed in the car, grateful for any help in getting closer to his destination. "You are really fortunate, you know," said the officer. "That cow you ducked behind and took the fall for you...that was no coincidence." The cop looked at the boy. "You hungry? There's a great little diner up ahead, just before the state line."

"That sounds perfect," the boy answered, his mouth beginning to water. "How do you know it wasn't a coincidence?"

"Well, I don't know for sure. But I don't believe in coincidences or chance; everything happens for a reason. Take that car, for instance. Just when you were about to get plowed by the bull, that car appeared and again took the fall for you. And it happened to be on the top of the hill. Were it further down on either side of the ridge, the driver likely would have had plenty of time to dodge him...and you could have been killed by the bull."

"Huh...maybe," the lad mused.

"Maybe? No, Something is looking out for you!"

"What do you mean, Something?"

"Well, God or no God, it appears that some—Thing—was protecting you."

THE ORPHAN DREAMER

"Did you get enough to eat?" the trooper asked while paying the bill.

"Yes, thank you so much for everything."

"Hey, what's in New Orleans, by the way?"

"I'm actually headed to Mexico, but that seems so far away still."

"Oh my, that is far, especially on foot." The cop took a sip of his soda and then laughed. "You going to Mexico to become a matador? Maybe that's why the bull was so angry at you!" The boy chuckled as well.

"Did you know bulls are actually color blind to the color red?" the trooper asked. "It's the movement of the matador's cape that provokes the bull; the color makes no difference. I think the color red is actually to trick the audience. People are easily duped!"

The cop stood and shook the boy's hand. "I've got to head back the other direction. I wish you well and stay safe."

As the orphan watched him through the window getting into his squad car, a robust gentleman slid into the booth the cop had warmed. "Pardon me, but I overheard part of your conversation."

The boy turned his attention to the intrusive man. "Which part?"

"The part about you traveling to Mexico. I'm headed to New Orleans myself. I could drive you there if you'd like."

The man felt sorry for him, the boy perceived. How he hated when people showed him pity. It made him feel inferior and special in an unfavorable way, almost as if he was less of a person than the one extending sympathy. But he needed a ride, so he would allow it and gratefully accept the kindness offered.

Maybe some Thing *is* guiding and looking out for me, the lad considered. Opportunities keep surfacing and drawing me

63

closer to realizing my dream. Perhaps I will discover my purpose after all.

"I would love that, thank you."

The sports car roared to life as the hefty man revved the engine. The orphan eased into the passenger seat and strapped his seatbelt on. "Good afternoon, passengers," announced the burly man. "This is your captain speaking."

The boy examined the man's face with a bewildered glare. Swinging his head around to confirm the empty back seats, he returned his gaze to the driver seat. "You feeling okay?"

"I feel terrific! Please remain in your seats and keep your seatbelts fastened until the seatbelt sign is turned off. I want to wish you all a safe and prosperous journey ahead."

"Um, maybe I don't need a ride after all," the lad said nervously as he reached for the door handle.

"Don't be silly, you need not worry! For I...am an airline pilot," he smirked.

"Oh, that makes more sense. You should lead with that information next time."

"I don't blame you for being cautious. There are lots of nuts out there. I tell you, flying planes has given me a different viewpoint toward people."

"How so?" the boy asked.

"Well, I've flown all over the place and people are largely the same throughout the world. I mean, there are all types of people, but a commonality with so many are that we are proud. I can say that because I used to be an arrogant man. Why I was so egotistical, I'll never know. But I thought I was all that: I was young and fit, I meet attractive women wherever I travel, and people have a high respect for pilots for some reason. Now I'm older and less fit, and I see the younger generation behave as I once did." The man looked up into the sky a moment through the windshield. "I guess one day I had a revelation. My eyes were opened."

"You became a Christian?" the boy inquired with intrigue.

"Oh, gosh no! Christians are some of the proudest people out there, not to mention, judgmental! No, I wouldn't say I'm a believer—in God. But I do think there's a higher Power… somewhere."

The orphan's interest dimmed. "I thought you had a revelation?"

"Yes, it was sort of an epiphany, I suppose. Did you know that during a typical flight, you are only seven percent of the distance to the edge of space? I tell you, years of gliding five miles in the air offers a unique perspective on the world. Entire cities shrink into neighborhoods, while neighborhoods are but a dot. And then people—you can't even see people! I'm a good-sized man, and I am nothing at that height. It's very humbling when you think about it. And yet, this minuscule, insignificant man that I am, was so conceited. And for what? I finally realized that I exist on no merit of my own. And any ability that I have, whether to move, talk, think, or reason are none that I myself obtained. Any talents and faculties of mind were granted to me. So I determined that I must be humble—that I must remain grounded—if you will."

The boy understood his play on words and what he was saying, but was perplexed. "How can you not believe in God if all that you are was gifted to you?"

"There must be a supreme Power, a deity, or who knows what," he affirmed and then took another glance in the sky. "But I simply cannot wrap my mind around the idea of a sovereign God who created us."

The boy perked up and gained some wind. "It sounds like you may have a greater faith in *not* believing in a God than if you did."

The orphan recalled books he had previously read on space and stars. "We live in a bubble on this earth. Don't you find it odd that the earth and other stars, planets, and moons are spherical? And every side of the earth is as if we were right side up and the remainder of the world were not? And yet gravity secures us here so we don't drift off. Imagine if we had no gravity, if even for a minute."

"So what are you suggesting?" the pilot asked.

"I'm not sure there's a God either, but the design of all things seems too perfect to have materialized by chance."

"I've wondered about that, too," the man said. "You know, if there is a God, I assume we'll meet him one day when we die."

"Yeah, I suppose," the boy agreed as he leaned over and peeked at the speedometer. "Maybe we should slow down a little. I'd rather not meet him today."

The man laughed. "For years, I've been transporting people from one place to their destination, and generally back again on their return flight. If there is an afterlife, I presume we are each transported from this world to the next...but never back again, of course. I find it fascinating that no one is ever able to return to warn us on what lies ahead. Once gone, forever gone to another—"

THE ORPHAN DREAMER

"I grew up in a convent," the boy interrupted, "and they taught us that when the body perishes, the spirit simply moves on to an alternate dimension, abandoning the physical body to rot and return to dust. The Book tells of some who will be given a new body in the next life."

"Okay, this conversation grew morbid quickly," the pilot said, eager to change the subject. "Speaking of bodies perishing, did you know the black box on an airplane isn't black at all? It's really bright orange, so it can easily be found."

"Let's hope they never need to find yours," said the boy.

"I hope not. But you know, flying high in the air is worth the risk to me…like speeding down the highway at present. It gets your adrenaline going."

"So you enjoy going fast, I see."

"It's more like, I have a difficult time going slow," the pilot clarified. "I'm passionate about flying, and I suppose, about driving fast. Work's not so bad when you love what you do."

The boy pondered the man's words before responding. "Sometimes it's tricky, though, knowing what's worth doing and what might simply lead to failure."

"I've learned you'll regret the things you *didn't* try more than those you did," the man replied. "Have the courage to achieve what you want to accomplish. Rarely are there shortcuts, and rarely do good things come easily. You must be willing to do the difficult work. Besides, that's where we get our sense of accomplishment: from the challenge."

The lad nodded his head in agreement. "I know you're right. I just don't want to make mistakes."

"You will certainly make mistakes! But accept the trouble and setback as part of life. And don't ever, ever give up."

"There are so many possible paths, so many options," the lad sighed, a bit overwhelmed. "Where does one begin?"

"My advice to you: discover your passion in life. Only then are you able to pursue your dreams. Then you will find inspiration and the confidence necessary to realize your vision. And don't be surprised if you encounter hope and love...and purpose along the way."

The orphan was glad to be pursuing his dream, and felt optimistic in his path thus far. "But what if I never learn my purpose?"

"Without purpose, a person will endure unhappiness and a sense of emptiness inside. And if nothing is done to deal with these emotions, loneliness and depression loom close behind."

The boy agreed; he would need to determine his purpose. Already a companion with sorrow and isolation, a welcomed change would be refreshing. Closing his eyes, he leaned back and dreamt of a hope renewed.

ELEVEN

The slight jolt of the car coming to a halt awakened the orphan. "We made it," said the pilot. "I have family just north of here, so this is where we must part, I'm afraid."

Though the sun had recently risen, smoky gray clouds blocked it from sight. "Where are we?" asked the boy sluggishly, surveying the unfamiliar surroundings.

"Welcome to New Orleans, the most unique city in America! This is Canal Street. They initially planned to build a canal right here years ago, but settled on a street instead. If you walk just a few blocks south, you'll hit the French Quarter, the oldest neighborhood in town. There you'll find lots of restaurants, hotels, bars...well, I suppose you're too young for those. Anyway, a few blocks further and you'll be swimming in the Mississippi River."

The boy opened the passenger door and stepped out. Turning and crouching to see the man once more, he said, "I really appreciate the ride."

"It's what I do, transfer people from one place to another. Do you need any money for food?"

"No, I have plenty," he replied and closed the door. The orphan didn't want to lie, but neither did he wish to be pitied. While thankful for the man's generosity, he had inconvenienced him enough. And though he had no money left at all, he would find a way.

As the pilot drove away, the boy immediately noticed a heavily populated cemetery across the street, on the way to the French Quarter. He crossed over and felt drawn to enter the old burial ground. The sky darkened as he did so, with clouds swelling and thunder rumbling in the distance. Like a miniature city, the graveyard was laid out with massive above-ground tombs and mausoleums. He meandered through a maze of tiny crumbling streets, curious of the thousands of souls laid to rest all around him. People strive to remain youthful and healthy, but in the end, we all die. It's inevitable.

Suddenly, a huge granite headstone, perhaps thirty feet tall, caught his attention. The engraving upon it spoke of a man named Alexander Milne who moved to New Orleans from Scotland in the late 1700s. Amassing a great fortune, he dedicated most of his wealth to establish orphanages for both boys and girls upon his death. Fearing his orders may be disregarded, his wishes were engraved upon his tomb.

An elderly gentleman drifted in effortlessly, more swiftly than a man his age and stature ought to be able. "What do ya think?" the aged man asked.

"Who are you?"

"I'm the groundskeeper…been here a long, long time."

"I've never seen anything like this," the orphan responded. "Why aren't the bodies buried in the ground?"

"Oh, you're not from around here, are you?"

"No. I'm from up north."

"Ah, well you're definitely in the South now," the old man laughed shrewdly. "Much of the town is below sea level, so the dead are buried above ground. With such a high water table, graves used to fill with water, causing buried caskets to float back up to the surface. I presume people didn't like seeing family members returning before their appointed time."

The hair on the boy's arms stood on end, and yet, he was fascinated. "No, that would be terrifying, to say the least."

"But take your time, look around. All types are entombed here: politicians, soldiers, musicians, pirates, and scores who died from plagues so long ago." The elderly man emit another devious laugh. "Some believe these cemeteries are haunted."

The boy peered down the long, dilapidated path paved between countless tombs. "But what do *you* think?" he asked, turning back to the groundskeeper. But the keeper was no longer present, so the boy resolved to leave at once and continue his way southward.

A brief three block jaunt led the lad directly to another cemetery. The sign out front boasted that it was the oldest and most renowned resting place in New Orleans. Opened in 1789, the location was chosen because it was well outside the city limits at the time. With years of growth, it is now bound on the edge of the French Quarter in the center of town.

Once again, the boy was lured within the gates to wander down the disintegrating cement trails amongst the tall tombs. The clouds threatened rainfall as he heard a faint, distressful singing up ahead through the dark and narrow passage. Mausoleums were cracked and crumbling on both sides of the ominous pathway. Some constructed of masonry had shed bricks on all sides, with weeds and gristly plants growing through the vault doors. Wrought iron fences disintegrated around numerous tombs, once offering an intimate perimeter, but now abandoned indifference.

An old woman of skin and bones was dancing before a battered and neglected tomb. Her chanting was anything but pleasing, and sounded more like sorcery in an unknown dialect. Nearby statues leaned mystically, crippled with missing heads and limbs. The boy quietly advanced until several feet behind her when she abruptly stopped her dance and chant. She remained completely still, facing the tomb, and after a moment, began yelling toward the humble dwelling of the departed.

Suddenly, she spun her head around like an owl, swiftly and with a cracking pop of her neck. Her eyes were gaping and furiously wild, and with a long mangled finger, she cursed toward the orphan. "Go back from where you came! You don't belong here!"

THE ORPHAN DREAMER

The lad was stricken with fear and took steps back. "There is death on your journey ahead," she warned. "Turn around now!" The witch shooed him away with violent gestures "Return or surely die!" she yelled.

As the boy swung around and began pacing hastily in the opposite direction, he perceived the woman shadowing him. He broke into a run with the witch scurrying only steps behind. Down the dingy and fractured concrete path he dashed until he saw the gated entrance. Glancing back once more, he noticed she was no longer following. So he returned his attention to the open gate and discovered the disfigured woman standing in the center of the entrance immediately before him. He tried to stop, but it was too late, and instinctively placing his arms out, he plowed right into her. They tumbled to the ground and lay next to each other in the dirt. The woman leaned in close and grabbed the boy's face with one withered hand, and with the other she pointed a shriveled finger at his reckless birthmark. "You are cursed," she shrieked and spit in his face.

He got up faster than ever and sprinted out of the graveyard until he arrived on Bourbon Street in the French Quarter. Stopping to catch his breath in front of an outdoor cafe, he thought about all the people who had bullied and laughed at him over the years, but never with such hostility as this woman and for no apparent reason.

"Have a seat," said a pudgy man, a dozen feet from the boy. The man slid a chair out from his table. "Best latté in town... join me!"

"I've never had one, but I'll try anything," the boy replied, still panting for air.

"What are you so out of breath for anyway?"

"An old lady...she was chasing me in the cemetery."

"Why on earth would she do that?" the portly fellow asked.

"I'm not sure. She was chanting and dancing strangely in front of a tall tomb. Then she saw me and freaked out...got really angry at me."

"Ah, yes. Every town has their share of spooks. She is one of those here." The boy's coffee was brought to the table, and before the waitress disappeared, the man ordered another coffee with extra heavy cream. "Don't mind her though," the man continued. "Practically every day she visits the graveyard and talks to the Voodoo Queen who lies in that tomb."

"She talks to the what?" asked the boy.

"The Voodoo Queen...that's what people call her. Her name was Marie Laveau. She died a century ago, but some believe she has magical powers, even from the dead." The lad sipped on his hot coffee and listened intently. "The Voodoo cult began in Africa and was brought here by way of slavery. It basically spread throughout the hurricane corridor, from western Africa through the Caribbean, especially from Haiti to New Orleans. Once here, it got mixed up with Catholicism. Anyway, various deities are worshiped, including the Grand Zombi."

"The Grand Zombi?" The boy couldn't believe what he was hearing. "Do you believe she has magical powers?"

"I'll tell you what I think," said the heavy man. "The Voodoo Queen died many years ago, just as you and I one day shall. She's still there, buried and unable to resurrect herself. Magical powers? Sorry, I can't place my faith in someone rotting in a grave."

He took a drink and casually admired the other diners relaxing around them outside. "Everyone has faith, misplaced or not, and places their hope in something or someone. But if that someone lacks power over death, what hope is there in that? I find it interesting that all founders of the world's religions have died and remain dead—all but one, that is, if what was penned is true: that one was resurrected who promises one day to return and resurrect others."

The boy pondered these words for a minute. "Then if what you say is true, there is no hope for anyone...unless what was written is in fact, true."

"Precisely," the man agreed. "Take New Orleans: Festivals are celebrated here literally almost every weekend. You can forget about your past, your present, and you can dress up in a costume. You can be whomever you want, hiding behind a mask if only for an evening, and free yourself from burdens and humdrum jobs and mundane life. People will accept you, there's no fear of rejection. Everyone is simply looking for happiness and love and hope."

The orphan relished the idea of wearing a mask and being accepted by everyone. But real life proved otherwise. "I wish I could wear a mask permanently," the boy confessed and finished his coffee. "I'm often rejected because of this." He turned his head to the right to emphasize his offensive birthmark.

"Listen," the man spoke up authoritatively while taking hold of his coffee mug. "Things don't always turn out the way you want them to, and that can be a good thing. You must look for opportunity in the flaws of life." Suddenly, the man's coffee cup slipped from his grasp and the little bit of coffee remaining spilled over onto the table. The boy grabbed his napkin to help clean up the mess, and within a few seconds, the waitress brought a wet rag to finish up.

"You can't please everyone," he continued. "Some won't like you and that's okay. Oftentimes, the one who is rude or abusive is dealing with their own issues and simply projecting them onto you. Remember, it's not always about you. You are not the center of the universe. Others are struggling with themselves, so don't take their insults personally."

The waitress returned with a fresh latté for the man and wandered off. "See there? A complimentary latté even though mine was cold and near empty. As one door closes, another one opens."

The boy sat motionless for a moment, visibly impressed as he surmised that the man spilled his coffee intentionally. "Does that always work? I mean, does another door always open as one closes?"

"Always," the man affirmed. "But you must remain alert, or you will fail to recognize it." He paused a few seconds, and then added, "Most people miss it. I learned that from my old boss down at the shipyard years ago."

"Shipyard? Where's that?"

"It's only ten or so blocks from here," the man pointed toward the Mississippi River. "I used to load cargo ships there. Hard work...I was much younger and leaner back then."

"Where do the ships transport the cargo?" asked the boy.

"Oh, all over the place; frequently straight through the Gulf toward Mexico."

The orphan thrust his bistro chair back at once and stood up. "Thanks for the coffee!" he said excitedly and bolted away.

TWELVE

An hour later, the boy made his way to the main office of the Port of New Orleans. He inquired if any cargo ships were headed to Mexico any time soon. In two days time, they replied, crossing the Gulf of Mexico to Veracruz. Pulling his map from his backpack, he observed that the city is located near central Mexico. Perfect, he supposed, for he was not yet certain of the whereabouts of the healing pool he needed to find. Once there, he could ask around and then direct his course in the appropriate direction. But one thing he was sure of: crossing the Gulf would save him valuable time in reaching his destination. "Any chance I can get a ride to Veracruz?" he asked.

"No, sorry kid," the office manager replied. "We don't do that here."

"I would stay out of the way, and I could help whenever needed," the boy urged with hope in his eyes.

"Again, sorry, but we have no use for you. Besides, you're too young."

The orphan showed himself out and wandered the streets all afternoon in loneliness. He felt shunned and detached from the world, even while the town around him teemed with people. His stomach growled. The coffee was pleasant earlier, but he was not offered food at the cafe and he had no money. Only hours prior, he was excited about the chance to sail over to Mexico. But that quickly led to discouragement. Better to keep expectations low in the future, he decided.

Anyway, he was used to rejection. I wish I had a different life, he thought. Others have it much easier. He knew it was unhealthy to flounder in self-pity, but something about doing so felt gratifying. Feeling sorry for himself in an unfair world offered an odd sense of comfort.

A weary sun rested as nightfall assumed control of the town. The boy found his way back to Bourbon Street as city lights burst with illumination. Vehicles were not allowed on the street in the evenings, as thousands came out to celebrate in the roads with live music, drinking, and revelry. People danced outdoors to swinging jazz music as cafes and pubs sprang to life. The road bustled with a multitude of every type and all ages. Many souls who were miserable only hours earlier had long forgotten the reason for their sorrows. A tipsy crowd strolling through the middle of the road parted for the right-of-way of a parade celebrating who knows what.

The orphan didn't care about any of it. The more congested the streets grew with people, the more isolated the boy felt. He ambled through the street amidst a sea of party goers. Local artists and musical performers lined the walkways peddling their talents for tips, and piano bars rallied to enliven spirits. He passed hotels, restaurants, and bar after bar, his spirits sinking lower and lower. Finally, he sat down on a slab of curb as a throng of people skirted around him on each side.

Observing the Spanish and French style architecture around him, he pondered his journey and the whimsical sounding names of the places he had traveled. He had passed through the Big Apple, the city with the largest population in the country. From there, he briefly visited the City of Brotherly Love and then the Big Peach. And now he sat in the middle of the Big Easy. What a laid-back lifestyle New Orleans seemed to offer compared to that of the constant hustle of New York City.

It was getting late and the lad was hungry and scared. No money, no family, and no friends. Doubts and regrets haunted him for having left the convent. Never had he gone hungry and he always had shelter and a place to lay his head. His eyes watered. He would need a job to survive by himself, but who would hire him? How would he afford a place to live?

It was a mistake to have left on his own, even considering the abuse and neglect. Tears streamed down his cheeks. Nobody seemed to notice him as they passed by on the street and sidewalk. It was bitter sweet. He usually didn't want people to notice him, but now no one did and he wished that someone would stop and help.

A few minutes later, the boy wiped his face. He remembered what the blind woman on the bus advised: the more grateful you are, the more beauty you will witness around you. She urged to see the positive in every circumstance. He did have much to be thankful for, he decided, and he knew that comparing himself with others was a thief of joy—jealousy is all consuming.

A few people were still out drinking and yelling; most had returned home. Trash gently blew down the near vacant roads, and a handful of drinkers were passed out along the pavement in contorted postures. Finding a comfortable bench on Bourbon Street, the lad lied down. Tears welled in his eyes once more. He looked up to the sky and softly spoke, "God, if you do exist, help me, though I know I don't deserve it. If you are real, show yourself to me. Grant me your provision, I pray."

The sun was beginning to climb, casting heavy shadows along the still and silent street. A ray of sunshine graced the boy's face to awaken him. Easing off the bench, he stretched, and by the soreness of his back, he realized the bench was less comfortable than he had originally believed. Walking down the Bourbon sidewalk, he noticed some the same lifeless bodies were still heavily sedated and strewn about. It was an apocalyptic scene, void of life and replete with trash everywhere.

Two blocks further, as the sun rose higher and shadows sunk lower, something caught the boy's attention just ahead in the curb cut along the street. Amidst empty beer cups and crumpled up flyers, a sparkle seduced the boy nearer. Something glittered in the debris, enlivened by the sun, reflecting beauty amidst rubble. Bending down to pick it up, the boy couldn't believe what he had uncovered. A gold ring with a single diamond in the center! The wedding ring must have slipped off someone's finger last night during the festival.

THE ORPHAN DREAMER

Standing there staring at the brilliant piece of jewelry, he hardly noticed the street sweeper creeping up behind him. His attention was suddenly riveted by the noisy truck as it passed alongside him, and he hurriedly placed the ring in his pocket. He watched as the street cleaner swept trash and filth into the giant hopper attached to the truck.

If the truck had arrived one minute sooner, I never would have seen the ring, he realized. It would have vanished before I had a chance to see it. Or if I had slept a minute longer, it would have been too late. Then he recalled his prayer the night before: for God to help and provide, and to show himself real. Was this an answer to prayer? he wondered. He observed the street sweeper shrinking smaller and smaller down the road. Or was it mere coincidence? People do have strokes of luck every now and then; coincidences do happen once in a while. He likely would have found the ring on his own had he not bothered to pray, he decided.

At any rate, he was glad to have found the ring. Now he could eat and have money to continue his journey! He searched many blocks before finding a pawn shop. It was still closed so he waited for it to open. Not wanting to appear desperate for the sale, he lingered a block away and hesitated for half an hour after it opened. Finally entering the shop, he glanced around initially. There was so much random stuff. At one time, he mused, each item was certainly appreciated, even adored, by its owner, but over time grew mundane. Do all material things end up in this manner in the eyes of the possessor, only to desire something more, something better? he wondered. Does it ever cease, the yearning for something grander?

The boy pulled the ring from his pocket and set it on the counter. "Ah, a wedding ring!" exclaimed the young pawn shop employee. "You don't look old enough to have been married."

"It's been in the family for some time," the lad responded casually, as if he wasn't sure he wanted to sell it. "I'm just curious what I might get for it."

"No worries. I never make it personal where anything comes from anyway. It's none of my business, and it's better if I don't know."

Upon examining the ring under a magnifying glass for some length, the pawn shop worker said, "I can offer you $400."

The orphan lacked the luxury of time, but he knew it was worth much more. "I was really hoping for at least $800," he countered as he picked up the ring. He would sell it for less, but was attempting to call his bluff.

"I'll tell you what. I'll give you $600 cash right now, no questions."

"Deal," the boy agreed and they shook hands.

The boy made his way to the Mississippi Riverwalk a few blocks from Bourbon Street and dined on a breakfast of hot coffee with milk and powdered sugar beignets. Never before had he seen a square donut without a hole in the middle. But they were delightful, especially having not eaten for over a day. He never would have experienced these had he not embraced this adventure. After eating his fill, he ordered five dozen more beignets and strolled down the Riverwalk toward the Port of New Orleans.

By the time he arrived at the port's main office, his arms were weary from carrying the beignets. He presented his offering to the office staff and explained, "I would've brought coffee, too, but I have only two arms."

THE ORPHAN DREAMER

They were ecstatic for someone bringing them doughnuts. "I remember you. Thank you so much!" said the port manager. "And we have coffee here already, come join us!"

And that he did, for though he was full, he wished to be courteous and found room for another beignet.

A phone rang and someone in the far corner of the room answered it. "The kitchen help is sick and can't make it in tomorrow," she told the manager, who informed the ship captain.

"Are you serious?" the captain replied, more than somewhat annoyed. He stuffed an entire beignet in his mouth and glanced at the orphan.

The boy sat up straight and grinned. "When one door closes, another one opens," he affirmed the captain.

The manager and ship captain trudged to the office and shut the door. Five minutes later, the captain reappeared and looked straight at the boy. "Okay. We leave tomorrow morning, eight a.m. sharp."

The orphan was learning to listen: opportunity knocks very softly sometimes. Later that evening, he dined on spicy crawfish, potatoes, sausage, and corn on the cob. It was the first time in his life to ever see or taste crawfish! What a world is out there, he thought. He felt encouraged again to have left the convent. More dangerous the world may well be, but he determined he would rather die while living than live restrained. Tomorrow, he would ship off into the Gulf toward Mexico. His dream was becoming reality.

83

THIRTEEN

Excitement surged within the orphan as the ship parted the dock of New Orleans. It was his first time on a ship and his first time to leave the country! He felt fortunate to be a kitchen helper and deckhand during the expedition, and while he would earn no pay, he would receive complimentary lodging, food, and a cruise to Mexico. He would arrive in Veracruz in five days and still have money to travel from the sale of the diamond ring.

The entire crew welcomed him aboard, seventeen members including himself. There was a captain, an executive officer, two kitchen stewards, three engineers to ensure a smooth running ship, and a number of deckhands and officers who oversaw the decks and maintained safety systems. The boy learned that his duties would include helping in the kitchen, cleaning, and running errands whenever needed.

His minimal cabin was perfect for the short jaunt across the Gulf. Upon entering, he observed two twin beds separated by a narrow end table, a shower, a desk, and an athletic young man in his mid-twenties seated at the desk. He was reading a thick book, but immediately looked up. "You must be the roommate," he said with a heartfelt smile parting a husky beard.

"I've heard about you. We're just a couple of vagabonds, you and I!"

"I don't know what a vagabond is," the boy admitted while setting his backpack on the floor. "But I suppose we're roommates."

"You and I are sort of lonesome drifters in a way, trailblazers in search of direction and purpose. I'm an evangelist throughout Mexico. I hopped on board as you, to help out as a deckhand for the passage across."

"An evangelist?" asked the boy, laying on his bed for a quick rest. "Why spend your life for such little pay for a people you don't know?"

"Fair question," he said and spun around in his chair. "I would gladly die as a missionary for the sake of the cause. Consider the disciples of Jesus. Each witnessed firsthand the miracles and resurrection of Christ, and all but one were murdered for their faith. Think about it: many people *do* die for a lie, but those die believing the lie to be true. People don't die for a *known* lie. They will rather cave in the face of death. The disciples, however, they saw their resurrected leader and never backed down. Knowing the truth firsthand, they willingly gave their lives."

"So, you're my roommate?" asked the orphan. "I'm not gonna...I don't know, wake up dead or something, am I?"

The missionary laughed and then slid his finger nonchalantly across his neck from one side to the other.

"Matthew, Paul, and James the Greater were beheaded. Andrew and Philip were crucified. Peter was also crucified, but upside down. Thomas was speared and burned alive, Matthias was stoned, and Bartholomew was skinned before being crucified. Thaddaeus was beaten to death, Simon the Zealot was sawn in half, and James the Lesser was cast from the Temple and then his head bashed with a club."

"Okay, that was kind of graphic," the orphan responded. "Why in the world do you know all that?"

"Because for me," the missionary expressed solemnly, "that's one of the clearest evidences that the resurrection actually occurred."

"Wait, you said all but one was murdered for their faith. So one did give in?"

"No, none of them did. John was boiled in oil, but he survived, and was exiled to the island of Patmos. Interestingly, that's where he wrote the book of Revelation."

"I struggle with faith," the lad confessed while staring at the ceiling. "I want to believe, but I'm somewhat indifferent right now."

"It took a gruesome season for me to fully surrender my life a couple of years ago. I was desperate and hopeless. I'm confident, few souls will turn when everything is going well for them. People lack the urgency and perceived need to be saved; they already feel comfortable and safe. But it's a sham; a thin veil clouds their reasoning."

"I suppose you're probably right. But I've been burned by the Church. It's full of hypocrites."

"You're not wrong there," replied the evangelist. "That's why you don't place your hope in people. You will always be disappointed." He picked up the book he was reading. "You must place your hope in the truth. It never changes."

THE ORPHAN DREAMER

After serving stew and bread to the crew members, the missionary and orphan sat at a table by themselves to eat dinner. "We should arrive in Veracruz in four days," said the boy.

"Yes, it will go fast," the evangelist replied. "Did you know that Veracruz literally means *True Cross*? A man named Cortes landed in Mexico in the 1500's and established the city. It was initially named Villa Rica de la Vera Cruz due to the gold in the area, and because he landed on Good Friday, the day Christ was crucified."

"No, I didn't know that. I originally planned to travel around the Gulf and go through Corpus Christi—"

"Ah, Corpus Christi...the *Body of Christ*," the evangelist interrupted.

"Why are there so many references to God and religion wherever one travels?" the boy asked while grabbing more bread. "I rode through Philadelphia, the City of Brotherly Love, where they hoped people would tolerate all religions."

The missionary wiped stew from his manicured beard. "Humans are needy. That's how God created us, to need him. Apart from him, there is a void and loneliness. It's the reason people all over the world are searching for truth, for the meaning of life."

"To be honest," the boy interjected, "I often feel like something is missing. I can't explain what it is, but I have a longing for more."

"That's normal. Only God can fill that void. All people groups in the world serve a god of some type. From the largest

87

cities to the most reclusive tribes: all share a desire and need, instilled by the grand Designer, to serve a higher power. Now granted, many are confused and remain far from the truth. But all are searching to fill a vacuum."

The boy walked to the counter and ladled more stew for himself. "But aren't there many truths, depending upon what each people group believes?"

"There is only one truth. One truth set against an opposing truth, by the very nature of the word and meaning of truth, can not stand. Two systems of belief boasting conflicting truths are divided against one another and may not both be true."

The following afternoon, after his chores were complete, the orphan went to the upper deck of the ship to get some sun. He peered out across the waters, scanning the horizon miles and miles into the distance. How vast the seas are with such endless volumes of water, he contemplated. A world wholly uncommon to his own, with terrifying depths below the surface. He pondered how little land exists upon the earth, and of that, much is ice and snow and desert. Every animal and fish is so uniquely designed than any other, where creatures of land have lungs and those of the ocean require gills for survival. He imagined how sorely disadvantaged the lunged beasts are to remain on dry ground, and the near non-existence of life above the watery expanses covering most of the earth.

Suddenly, a whale surfaced not too far from the ship. A couple of other shipmates noticed as well and alerted the others. "It's a blue whale!" exclaimed an officer to the orphan. "That is a very rare occurrence in the Gulf of Mexico. I have never seen one in this area before today. You must be good luck!"

The boy's eyes followed the sea creature swimming alongside the ship, rising to the surface now and then to inhale fresh air through its blowhole. "I forgot that whales have lungs as we," the boy said.

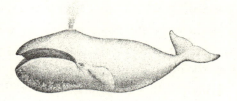

"Yes, amazing beast! That's the largest animal on the planet, maybe ninety feet long, right in front of you."

The beast withdrew from the side of the ship and descended deep into the waters and out of sight. The orphan searched and searched, but he never saw it again. Much life occurs in the world beyond the reach of the eye, the boy reflected.

That evening, back in their quarters, the orphan told the missionary about the behemoth whale. "I've never seen anything like it!" he said excitedly. "It was surreal; I may have thought it was my imagination had no one else been there to see it. How could such a creature evolve from nothing?"

"It couldn't. From an ant to the whale, and all in between: everything was created for a particular purpose."

Every muscle in the boy's face relaxed as he plunged into deep thought. "You seem to have it all figured out. I wish that I knew my purpose."

"I'll tell you a secret: I don't have it all figured out," the evangelist replied. He thought for a moment and then continued. "There's an old story I like about a man who lived by the sea. God gave him a purpose one day, a special calling for only him to perform. But he refused, and instead, he boarded a ship traveling in the opposite direction he was supposed to go. A violent storm arose and the sailors feared for their lives, tossing cargo overboard to lighten the load. When they believed they might all perish, they cast lots to determine who was responsible for this misfortune. The lot fell upon the man running from God, and the sailors questioned whom he was and what he had done to cause such trouble.

"'I worship the God of heaven,' he confessed, 'who made the sea and land, and I have resisted the will of God. Toss me into the sea and it will calm, for I know this adversity is my fault.' The sailors desperately tried rowing back to shore, but the more they rowed, the angrier the sea grew. Finally, they hurled the man overboard, and the sea became still. It's said that a fish or a whale swallowed the man. Certain whales, like you saw today, do open their mouths so wide that a man could possibly be swallowed if it could only manage to slip down its throat.

"Anyway, after three days and nights in the fish's belly, the man is said to have vowed to complete God's mission, and the fish vomited him onto dry land."

"That's disgusting!" the orphan chimed in. "If I was thrown up onto dry land, the first thing I'd do is get back in the water and wash off...but that's me."

"My point is that we each have a special purpose, a calling from God. For those who follow him, he helps and guides

THE ORPHAN DREAMER

along the way. But things get rocky and confusing when we turn away. Prosperity comes from living rightly and fearing God. His favor shines upon those who follow in his ways."

⌒

Early the following morning, the boy helped prepare breakfast in the galley. As crew members arrived for breakfast, he shoveled eggs, sausage, and toast onto their plates. One of the deckhands, who had mocked him before about his birthmark, received his food tray and looked at the head cook. "The freak didn't touch my food, did he?" he said with a nod to the orphan.

"Knock it off," the cook scolded the bully.

Upon sitting down, the same guy hurled his toast at the orphan from his seat and struck him in the face. The boy retained his composure, grabbed a fresh piece of toast, and approached the bully peacefully. "I think you dropped your toast," he offered politely. As his oppressor accepted the gift, the lad swung his right arm around and struck him on the cheek. While he didn't enjoy fighting, he learned early on to strike first before it's ever expected.

The bully jumped out of his chair and the boy tackled him to the floor. Seconds later, the orphan suffered three fists to the face before others separated the pair. Both were reprimanded by the captain and given filthy duties to perform that afternoon. "Next time we'll throw you both overboard! Just do your job!"

Early that night in their cabin, the boy confessed his insecurities with the missionary regarding his blemished face. "Listen, your birthmark does not define you, nor does any other imperfection you may have," the missionary advised.

91

"The heart defines a person. Your birthmark simply represents the blemish we each possess, the defects of the heart. No one is perfect—we're all flawed."

The orphan stood in front of the mirror in their room, pondering the reflection of his stained face. It always stared back at him defiantly, casting judgment and affliction upon him.

"God said that he knew you before he ever formed you in the womb, that he set you apart as unique and special. Everyone is insufficient and all need restoration with God. Whether one is an orphan or has cruel earthly parents, a perfect, loving Father exists and awaits, ready to provide and unleash his favor upon any who will turn to him."

"You don't understand," said the boy. "I don't deserve him. I've done things too shameful, too offensive to warrant his mercy."

The evangelist shook his head. "God already knows all your guilt. But he wants you to confess your wrongs, to admit them, and then turn from them. God is a real help in time of need, and he gives strength when one is weak. Never forget, you must humble yourself and bow at the foot of the cross—that is where your treasure will be found."

That last piece of advice weighed heavily on the boy's heart, as it was the same expressed by the pastor he lived with in Atlanta prior to his death. A few more insights were spoken by the missionary, but the lad failed to hear them.

The boy grabbed a blanket and told his cabin mate he needed some time alone. He climbed to the upper deck, spread out his blanket, and lay down beneath the clear night sky. The tapestry of stars was unbelievable in the darkness of the sea. Each star popped with such clarity and intensity like never before. The Orion constellation was still plainly visible. With summer approaching, it would soon be hidden for those in the northern hemisphere. He imagined himself again as a relentless Hunter, pursuing his dream and purpose, no matter the cost.

The solitude refreshed his senses as a cool gust blew across the ship and persuaded the whispering of waves. He cherished nature and how it prompted him to ponder the complexity of the world. He was always fascinated by the vastness of the universe and the orbit of planets around a stationary sun in flawless symphony: the rotation of the earth and the moon around it, together orbiting a sun anchored for the day and the moon for the night, the optimal distance of earth from sun fostering life and growth, the countless systems in the world promoting life in a constant barter of oxygen and carbon dioxide, and rain compelled by the passage of clouds and currents.

He reflected upon the universal standards of morality, of the human race discerning the disparity and conflict between right and wrong. A moral code we each possess, yet justify in breaching in the name of self interest.

The orphan was overwhelmed anew with a sensation of insignificance between the boundless sea and an endless stage of stars. If there was a God, why would he care for *me*? he wondered. Why would he give his life for mine? It made no sense. How could a sovereign God find value in me?

He fixed his gaze upon the stars of Orion again. Something about them made him feel safe and relaxed. They were familiar and dependable and governed with silent authority in the night sky. In a strange and nostalgic way, it seemed to extend the boy hope.

FOURTEEN

Once the freighter docked into the port of Veracruz, the boy thanked the crew members for the ride. The evangelist hugged the lad and promised he would pray for him on his travels. "Remember what we talked about," he urged. "God wants to be your Father. He awaits with open arms." That sounded nice to the boy, but he was still unsure if he needed that much commitment in his life right now. He had made it to Mexico and it was time to celebrate!

Slinging his backpack over his shoulder, he parted and began his hike past several other container vessels docked in the port. A smaller ship was being loaded from two military trucks littered with armed guards. Boxes were off-loaded by dollies and transferred to the ship in an orderly fashion. The men were efficient and rigid, as if meeting a strict deadline. Two of the armed men glared at the boy, and one of them shooed him away. They looked suspicious, to say the least.

Meandering through the streets of Veracruz most of the day, he finally spotted a vibrant cafe for dinner. If the locals approved of the food, he figured it must be good. Seated near an outdoor fire pit, he indulged on baked snapper smothered in a tomato sauce with capers, olives, and garlic. The fresh seafood and fusion of tastes was positively satisfying.

The boy found himself staring into the fire pit after his meal. The dancing flames and the crackling of burning pine animated his senses. Occasionally, sparks would float skyward and quickly vanish into the night. What an astonishing phenomenon—the mystery of fire—we take for granted, he thought. Its appearance and effects are unlike anything else in the world.

A moth was lured by the intense glow of the blaze, and it circled the pit to comprehend the anomaly. Around and around it encircled the leaping flames, seeking enlightenment in its new discovery. The light enticed the moth for some time, as it sought to enhance its life, perhaps, but in the end it impulsively dove into the flames. The boy's life flashed before him suddenly, and he wondered if he was nothing more than a moth.

He paid for the meal and left to find a modest hotel room for the night. On the way, he discovered an ice cream stand and that he had just enough room for dessert. He celebrated making it this far with a double scoop of chocolate rum fudge. He was learning to find joy in achieving small milestones along his journey in life.

Upon choosing a charming hotel, he made a point to speak with the lobby concierge first thing. "Excuse me. Have you ever heard of a healing pool in Mexico?"

The attendant squinted her eyes and looked above the boy's head in deep thought. "Now that is a random question, even for me. Yes, there are many healing pools and spas around here."

"No, not just any healing pool," the boy clarified. "It's a specific natural pool discovered years ago inside a limestone cavern."

"Oh, in a cenote…a sinkhole!" replied the concierge enthusiastically. "Why didn't you say so? I've never been to it,

THE ORPHAN DREAMER

but I've heard of one due east of here. The Temple of the Healing Goddess is there. It's very far away though, maybe eight hundred miles."

"Thank you for your help!" The boy retired to his room and unraveled the worn map from his backpack. He would leave in the morning and head southeast, around the base of the Gulf. Surely people could guide him the closer he arrived.

Sleeping in was a treat, especially in a comfortable bed in a room all to himself. After a late breakfast, the boy checked out of the hotel and hailed a cab out front. "Looks like rain soon," said the taxi driver. "Where you headed?"

"You speak English?" the boy replied, and fastened his seat belt.

"Fairly well. It helps as a driver, especially in a port town."

"I need to go about eight hundred miles east."

The cabbie took his foot off the gas pedal abruptly. "I'm sorry, I can only go fifty miles outside of Veracruz. I generally stay within the city. There's a town around there, though. I can drop you off and you can continue with another cab."

"No problem," said the boy. "I didn't think you could. And actually, I don't have enough money to get that far. The fifty miles will all but wipe me out."

The driver waved his hand in the air. "You'll make it to wherever you're going, kid. Don't worry about not having enough money. I've been poor my entire life, and I'm still here. Minimal funds are a blessing, not a curse. Nothing encourages creativity more than when you find yourself in need."

97

"I've found myself in need several times on my trip. I've made it this far somehow."

"You must live beneath your means," the cabbie advised. "A person grows with adventure, not from material possessions. Think about your past birthdays. Gifts received over the years become cloudy, if not forgotten, and yet, you retain memories of special experiences from those celebrations."

"That's a good point you make," the boy agreed. "I suppose a more meaningful memory is made in the mind."

"I have very little," the driver continued. "But I've seen so much. I've met many unique people, from all walks of life, many of whom were wealthy. It's sad though—the majority of them seemed so unsatisfied in life, almost empty inside."

"I can relate," said the boy. A light shower commenced and lightening neared as they sped through town. "Is it safe around here?"

"Relatively safe." The cabbie glanced up to see the lad in his rear view mirror. "Why, do you have many enemies?"

The orphan shrugged his shoulders. "The usual, I suppose." The boy felt less vulnerable talking about himself in a foreign country, to a man he would likely never meet again. "I'm learning that my biggest enemy is definitely myself: my fears, doubts, insecurities. I struggle with self-pity, loneliness, feeling worthless—"

"Okay!" the driver interrupted. "Well, you're honest, that's for sure! Where are you from?"

Leaving the city lights behind and the rainstorm strengthening, the surroundings darkened substantially. "I'm from way up north," the boy replied. "I'm on an important expedition."

THE ORPHAN DREAMER

"Well, if you're looking for girls, you've come to the right place. The most beautiful ones are right here. They make the best wives, too!"

The orphan was not amused. "No, I'm not looking for girls." He was on a mission and the prospect of a girl was the last thing on his mind. The cab was silent as lightening flashed violently with a loud crash of thunder immediately afterwards.

Life is full of choices, the boy considered. Countless girls from whom to choose, not simply one and if you miss that one you have altogether missed out. The same with occupations and places to live—opportunities and alternatives are almost limitless. If a God does exist, he reasoned, the person who lived appropriately and followed his ways was undoubtedly more inclined to choose wisely. God would bless his job, place of residence, or the girl he selects.

Flashing red lights glowed up ahead and landed upon the wet windshield. A quiet intersection had snuck up in the gloomy rural surroundings. There were no other headlights, nor brake or parking lights anywhere. It seemed they were alone on a backcountry road with no signs of life in sight. A blood red from the solitary traffic light oozed down the front glass as light refracted within each raindrop and streamed down the windshield. The boy was mesmerized by the distorted neon dripping down the window.

A few antiquated shops and buildings could barely be made out along the road as they passed the intersection. The cab driver slowed down as they neared a row of three tall speed humps in the street. Speeding over them quickly would certainly wreck havoc on an old car such as this one, possibly incapacitating it. As they slunk over the rumble strips, four guys with guns slung around their shoulders emerged from nowhere and stepped into the middle of the road. It resembled a routine

99

military checkpoint at the entrance of the meager town, but the driver knew better. They were criminals, posing as soldiers for corrupt gain. He sunk his foot on the gas pedal and jerked the steering wheel to swerve around the armed men.

Passing them by on the shoulder, one of the men yelled out and they opened fire. The orphan immediately ducked as low as he could below the seat. He heard glass shattering, metal smacking, and muted thuds in both the front and back seats. A brief squeal exhaled from the driver's seat and the cab rushed wildly off the road. Gunfire ceased, and after a couple of sudden bumps and hurdles, the car lunged into the front of an old building. Both the car and the rain died off in near unison.

The boy heard the men approach and open the driver's door. One began arguing with the others in Spanish, and the orphan perceived that the driver was dead. Suddenly the back door opened, and one of the men unbuckled the lad and pulled him forcefully from the car. On his way out, the boy noticed blood dripping down the windshield. He was shaken up and light-headed, but besides being bounced around and bumped on the head, he didn't observe any serious injuries on himself.

Binding his hands and feet, the men dragged the boy a block down the desolate road. A parked pickup truck awaited them in the shadows. Lifting him over the tailgate, they set him down on his stomach and pulled him further into the bed. His head was pulsating now as he stared at the murky floor of the bed beneath him. The cargo bed jolted seconds later and

THE ORPHAN DREAMER

something was pulled alongside him, grazing his shoulders and legs. He angled his head to the side and hardly recognized the lifeless body of the cab driver brushing up against him. His face was only inches from his own, and even in the dense darkness his mangled visage was horrifying. He could feel the corpse's blood on his cheek as it slowly channeled toward him along the truck bed, his face forging a dam in hindering the flow. The orphan turned his head the other direction to look away, clearing the dam and covering his other cheek in blood. The scent of death permeated the bed of the truck.

The boy observed one of the men accompanying him in the bed of the truck, his boots and gun barrel in his peripheral. He heard the three remaining guys crawl into the front of the truck, shut the doors, and drive away. Somewhat in shock, he was trying to make sense of what was happening. These were obviously corrupt men, but who were they and what did they want? They were definitely not military or police officers; most likely criminals attempting to either steal their car or else rob them for safe passage through town. They likely didn't expect the cab driver to flee, and possibly never intended to kill him. Stalling the car with bullets was probably their intention, and discovering the driver dead doubtlessly incited their argument.

But now they've seized the dead body and his own. What do they want with me? the orphan wondered. He pretty much was witness to everything, he reasoned, and knows they killed an innocent man. Of course they wouldn't let him go; he knew way too much. They would need to kill him to ensure their guilt disappeared along with him. The boy was trembling, but too traumatized to cry.

Thoughts came flooding to him, advice he had heard long before. Fear is almost always an illusion, nothing more. Besides, nothing good comes from worrying. It is worthless and unhealthy. Never waste time and energy fretting about things outside of your control.

He studied the cab driver's face next to him, his lifeless eyes open and bloody. This was certainly not an illusion! *And I get that worrying is harmful and vain, but what if there was something I could do. What if I could somehow control my circumstances?*

The pickup truck ran over a bump in the road, sending the boy's head in the air a couple of inches and smacking it back down against the metal bed. He looked again at the man's face next to him, as it shifted with each jolt of the truck. He had seemed like a nice enough man less than an hour ago, cheerful and content with life, but that was wrenched from him instantly.

He recalled the pastor's desperate warning to his congregation: do not wait to surrender your life to Christ, lest you die on the way home! The man lying beside him was clearly out of time to make a decision. That was it. He was hypothetically in heaven or hell at the moment, if either existed, and there was nothing he could do about it anymore.

But what did he have to live for, the boy reflected about himself, glancing at a bobbing gun barrel nearby. Perhaps he was better off dead. He had neither possessions nor home for which to return. Nobody would even miss him if he were gone. He resolved not to fight back if presented the opportunity. He was outnumbered, had little strength remaining, and had no weapon. He would leave it to God, if there was one and if he even cared, to either protect or allow him to die.

At last, the truck slowed to a crawl, turned slightly, and came to a halt. The boy heard other voices and the creaking of a metal gate in front of them. The pickup meandered slowly down a polished driveway. Struggling to look beyond the side of the truck bed, he noticed an enormous stone mansion towering in the sky, illuminating like an exhibit in a museum. They stopped again and shut the engine off.

A flurry of movement and heated conversations flared up all around. Men inspected the truck bed with flashlights, scrutinizing both bodies lying in a pool of blood. The boy felt like an animal in the zoo, only worse—more like an animal in a slaughterhouse—as he was tormented and most likely soon to be murdered. A heated exchange ensued between several of the men, arguing back and forth at length. Finally, an authoritative order was shouted, one of the men slapped the side of the truck, and it roared back to life and drove on. The smooth pavement swiftly morphed into a private gravel road. After passing two or three additional stone homes, the truck came to a stop.

Without delay, the tailgate was lowered and the lad's feet were unbound. Men assisted him out of the back of the pickup and led him down a dirt trail leading into a wooded area. He observed a number of smaller structures sprinkled around the property, all enclosed within a rustic rock wall. The perimeter walls were tall, and the boy supposed that he must be in a drug compound. With hands still bound, armed men escorted him through a winding path overlayed with trees. Faint lamps dotted the pathway until they arrived in front of a secluded habitation encased with thick stone walls.

This is where they will kill me, the orphan was certain.

Entering the double colonial front doors, lights flicked on and the boy found himself in a spacious game room. Billiard, shuffleboard, and foosball tables were arranged on the left side of the room, and a walk-in cigar humidor with leather sofa and chairs on the right. A lengthy bar was showcased in the center, brandishing a myriad of illuminated whiskeys in the background. They led the boy around the bar and behind a dividing wall separating the front from the back end of the building. A broad room opened up, dimly lit, harboring an enormous cage resembling a jail cell. Constructed with iron bars on all sides and a partition of bars in the center, it was perfectly dissected into two rooms, each the size of a modest bedroom.

A massive mountain lion unexpectedly appeared from the rear of one of the cell units and approached the front of the cage. A nervous chill shivered throughout the boy's body as he realized the manner of ruthless bloodshed used at the compound. These men were cold-blooded savages! They would murder him and feed his dead body to the cougar, or else lock him up with the animal and allow it to viciously tear him to shreds before devouring him.

The boy's heart pounded heavily as they neared the cougar's door. His head ached and he was exhausted. He tried to swallow, but his mouth was too dry. This was it: the end of his anguish, the end of his abuse, the end of his emptiness, his hopelessness, his insignificance. This was the end of his life.

Why would a God bless him with life, only to allow such misery and suffering? Others enjoyed proper lives comprised of family and friends, security and love.

He didn't care anymore. Life was cruel and unfair. The room was oscillating erratically and his knees buckled, toppling him to the floor. Two men hoisted him up as a third swung open a crudely creaking cell door.

Shoving him inside the spacious cage, he again collapsed and lay there, motionless. His wrists were unbound, and with eyes closed, he continued to sense the room shifting back and forth. The squeak of the cell door ended in a solid clamping of metal locking with metal. The boy heard the men leave and the shutting of the Spanish front doors. Opening his eyes, he raised his head and looked around. Realizing he was in an empty cell, he breathed a sigh of relief, and noticed the mountain lion pacing in the adjoining cell. He was relatively safe for now, he thought, at least until the lion's next feeding. With heavy eyes, he laid down his head and yielded to the sanctuary of sleep.

Lured to the restorative waters in the healing pool once more, the lad felt refreshed and invigorated. The beauty was radiant, promoting well-being as the cool waters purged all burdens away. Three Spanish ships smoked in the distance. He knew he was dreaming again, perhaps hallucinations due to his present trauma. Striving to comprehend, he supposed while others basked in lives of prosperity, he represented one of the ships destined for sorrow and misfortune…a life of lament and doom.

FIFTEEN

The orphan awoke to the metal clanging of his cell door. He saw no one, but somebody had definitely been there while he slept. A thick blanket was neatly folded and placed next to him, along with a water basin; a portable restroom was also positioned toward a rear corner of the cell. He crawled toward the panther's cell, who instantly arose and resumed its pacing. Cautiously extending his hand between the iron bars invoked the beast to charge and swipe his paw maliciously. The boy jerked his hand back, narrowly missing razor-sharp claws as they slashed at the metal bars. The lion appeared hungry and angry, and the boy would think twice before trying that again.

Before long, two armed men arrived, each carrying a tray. One unlocked the boy's cell door with a key, and held it open, while the other entered. Keeping a keen eye on the lad, he set down a platter of food and water. The lion smelled the food and was on high alert, observing every move they made. The man retreated, and they fastened his door before proceeding to the adjoining cell. Instead of entering the panther's cell, one of the men slid a tray of raw meat along the concrete floor through a gap fashioned specifically for the purpose. The animal wasted no time in ravaging his primitive feast, tearing muscle and crackling bones.

The men departed in haste, and the boy took a long drink and began eating his food. As he ate, he sat there and observed the wildcat destroying its prey. Halfway through his meal, the boy had a horrifying thought. Were they feeding the lion the remains of the cab driver? He couldn't be sure, but if they were, what happens when there was no more of the man's corpse? Would he be next, as they are merely keeping him alive to preserve his body for future meals? It made sense, he theorized: supplying cheap food while simultaneously disposing of bodies. There would be neither proof nor incriminating evidence of any foul play.

It oddly reminded him of an idea he had when he lived in the convent. With such cold winters, a person could easily murder someone with a thick, sharp icicle, and then leave the scene. The murder weapon would melt soon enough, and even if discovered before fully melting, fingerprints would be long gone. He felt this scenario with the lion was disturbingly similar.

Once finished, the panther came near the boy's cell and stood there staring at the lad. Inching closer, the boy again held his palm out toward the beast, only this time keeping his hand on his own side of the bars. The panther was infuriated, growling, hissing, and slashing his claws against the metal divider. At one point, the animal lunged and tried to bite the boy, squashing his face in between the bars with hopes of wedging through. Saliva slimed like honey from the lion's mouth to the floor. The boy backed away in fear and determined to give up in befriending the neighboring inmate.

The following day, the armed men brought more food, a tray for the boy and another for the lion. It was only one meal per day, but it was a sizable portion, and he fared better than other possible options he could imagine. The panther tried to attack him again, but beyond that and plenty of naps, there was little excitement. Still questioning whether the lion was dining on the cab driver, and if so, what might happen when the final morsel was digested, the boy devised a straightforward plan of escape. Time was waning and his window of opportunity would soon shut. He had seen too much, he knows too much; they would never let him go at this point.

As expected, the men arrived around the same time the next day with trays of food and water. One held open the door while the other set the meal down. It was highly risky, but he figured this was his best chance. While the man bent down to deliver the food, the boy grabbed the rifle hanging from his shoulder and yanked it hard. The gun strap easily slipped from the man's shoulder, but got caught on the gunman's wrist. He grasped the gun as well, and a tug of war ensued. The rifle whirled and twisted haphazardly, as they wrestled for control. A few random shots fired, a couple of them ricocheting off the iron bars. The second gunman scrambled into the chamber and struck the lad in the head with the shaft of his automatic rifle.

The boy slumped into the metal poles adjoining his cell with the next and tumbled to the cement floor. Crude words were cursed in Spanish as the two men kicked him several times in the chest and gut. "Next time, we shoot you!" one sternly warned. They slammed the cell door shut and left the lad lying in the fetal position.

The blow to the head left him dazed and disoriented. His head ached and vertigo set in with a loss of equilibrium. Sleep absorbed the strain of his trauma by suspending his mental and physical suffering; his body needed rest, not to mention healing. Most of the day passed by along the iron bars in virtually a comatose state, awaking only briefly now and then in confusion.

He dreamt that he had a loving mother who discovered him in his time of need. She doused a hand towel in warm water and gently swabbed his forehead, then his cheeks, and lastly his nose and chin. It felt good to have someone care for him and nurse him back to health. She dampened the cloth and wrung out the excess water onto the floor. He smiled as she again caressed his forehead and swabbed his hair over and over with the wet towel. Though he had never known anyone to tend to him in that manner, he found it somehow nostalgic.

The lad awoke to the tongue of the mountain lion caressing his forehead through the metal bars. His tongue was warm and coarse and felt like nothing he had ever known before, almost like dull, wet sandpaper. With each lick, the panther would rewet his tongue and resume lapping his hair and face. The boy didn't move and didn't care. He was no longer fearful of the beast. If it killed him, so be it.

But instead, it cleansed his wounded head. For some reason, it was moved by the cruelty rendered upon the boy. It was no longer the boy's enemy, no longer his rival. The cougar was extending compassion, the lad realized, more than most humans had ever lent. At last, the lion ceased lapping and stretched out against the dividing cell bars, alongside the boy. The lion perceives him the same as he, the orphan surmised. They were both caged against their wills and unkindly treated by malicious savages.

With tufts of fur protruding between the iron bars, the orphan carefully reached in and touched the panther's back. The wildcat swiftly glanced at his hand, observed it a few seconds, and calmly turned back and set his head down. Emboldened, the boy reached further into the adjoining cell and cautiously pet its back, then its neck, and then its head. He retracted his arm and ever so gently patted its rump. "See, you're not so bad," he confirmed.

The lion rolled over onto his back, legs draped against the bars. He wants a belly rub, the boy figured. As he began petting its belly, the wildcat closed his eyes in satisfaction. The cat hungered for affection the same as he, the lad realized, and in short time, they had built a mutual trust. They were presently one, in a way, enslaved companions now sharing a common camaraderie.

The boy cautiously held one of its front paws in his hand. It was enormous, larger than he had anticipated. The lion constricted its paw unexpectedly and its sharp claws extended far out, flaunting its deadly weapons. Seconds later, it retracted them and they disappeared deep within its fur. The orphan marveled. The animal's barbs are stored away when not needed, and easily protract when required for a climb or attack. It was science fiction sort of stuff, he supposed, such designs in nature we take for granted. Surely there must be a lofty Fashioner, or some manner of one anyway.

The boy finally ate his meal of the day, at least the edible portion, after it sat out all afternoon. Seated on the floor, he observed the mountain lion sleeping. It always slept. What more did it have to live for, except the inherent desire to be free and exist as wildcats were intended? He pondered the free will of mankind, to do as one chooses, whether to live morally or wickedly. Each has a choice, to do what is proper or else follow the dictates of his own heart, even if it proves corrupt.

How can so much evil endure in the world if there was a loving, caring God? Perhaps it's only for a time, he reasoned, as he allows man to live within his own discretion. Maybe he does use it all toward his good purposes, somehow in the grand scheme of things, as they taught in the convent. The notion

THE ORPHAN DREAMER

sounded pleasant, but he couldn't comprehend how many circumstances could ever be used for benefit.

Tears welled up in his eyes as he conceived no hope for freedom. The cartel could never let him go without jeopardizing their own interests. The sun plunged as he himself descended into a dark cave, desperate and hopeless. It was arguably the darkest night of his life. He sobbed uncontrollably, thick weighty tears trickling down his cheeks. He learned long ago that it's all right to cry, as it released unfavorable feelings and burdens. It was the natural outlet for the human body to channel sorrow toward a sense of serenity and guard it from complete mental breakdown. He wondered why animals lacked the capacity to cry. Maybe that's part of how God made man in his own image, with a depth of emotion foreign to animals. Then again, who can confirm the creation of man at all?

He remembered the words of the evangelist while on the cargo ship: "God is a help in the time of need. He gives strength when one is weak."

He wiped his eyes and looked toward a window past the iron cage. "If you are real, God, remove my fear and give me courage to get through this night. Inspire me, and while I don't deserve it, grant me help in my time of need. Show yourself real to me."

He stretched out alongside the dividing bars of the cell and drifted to sleep.

Early the following morning, as the sun began to ascend, the orphan was awakened by the soft voice of a young girl.

"Perdóname," she whispered. "Excuse me. Who are you and what are you doing here?"

The boy half-opened his eyes and answered groggily, "What do you mean, 'What am I doing here?' I don't want to be here. I was kidnapped!" He felt his head where he was struck by the rifle. It was aching and a sizable knot had formed.

"But why? And by whom?"

He stood up and staggered nearer the girl, blinking firmly a couple of times to see more clearly. Sunlight seeped in the few windows around the rear perimeter of the dwelling. The wildcat lifted his head in curiosity of the intruder before settling back down. "How long have you been here?" the girl persisted her questioning.

He had no idea what she said, or even if she had spoken. He had never seen anyone as lovely as she. For an awkwardly long moment he stared at the girl without realizing, as if time were suspended. Everything about her physically was appealing. Chestnut hair curled around her face, cheekbones and jawline in perfect symmetry. Her shoulders glistened a honey bronze, the petite sundress clinging to the girl's contoured form with waist and hips curving flawlessly.

She laughed aloud and broke the awkward silence. "You act like you've never seen a girl before!"

THE ORPHAN DREAMER

The embarrassed boy immediately regained composure. "I have, just not anyone like you." That sounded ridiculous, he realized right away.

"Okay, now you're being dramatic," she said with a flirtatious smile. But he wasn't being dramatic at all—at least, not intentionally. But more than anything, her dark chocolate eyes are what captivated him. Through them, it seemed he glimpsed her spirit.

"I…I was involved in a car accident," he explained. "They shot and killed my cab driver and brought me here against my will."

The girl's eyes widened as she listened. "Oh, my gosh!"

"I think they're feeding the dead driver to the lion," he added.

"I wouldn't doubt it," she replied. "My father is a very crooked man."

The boy studied her lips meticulously with each word she uttered. She spoke with grace and allurement. She caught him staring again. He instantly looked down in embarrassment.

"Oh…my…word!" the girl blurted in amazement, as she leaned in to examine the left side of his face. "Is that a birthmark?"

"Yes," he said faintly. The boy glanced at her and turned his head to conceal the blemish. An attractive girl like her would never fall for someone who looked as he did. She would never reciprocate his feelings. His only chance was to find the healing pool and have his face restored. But that was no longer an option.

"Your birthmark. You're going to think I'm crazy, but I've dreamt about it on occasion. A boy from a foreign land would one day come. I hadn't thought much of it until you—"

The boy turned back to her again. "You had dreams of a boy with a blotched 'X' across the side of his face?"

"Well, no, not an 'X'. But as you stared down it resembled a cross. I've had dreams of a boy with a cross on his face, precisely like yours, that would find me and guide me to my destiny. I know it sounds absurd."

"Not at all," he replied. "I, too, have had strange dreams. I'm traveling now—well, I *was* traveling—because of one those dreams, to locate a legendary healing pool in Mexico."

"There are numerous healing pools, at least rumored to possess healing powers," she said. "One in particular is highly regarded. I know where it is. I can take you there!"

He listened attentively. It sounded too surreal to be true. "How did you know I was in here, by the way?"

"I didn't. I heard gunfire yesterday. It sounded close. Plus, I thought I noticed someone carrying a tray of food out here—and not raw meat like usual!" She looked around nervously. "Listen, I shouldn't be here. I have to go, but I'll get you out of here, I promise. I'll find a key—"

"But what if you don't!" The orphan was not convinced at all. "What if you're too late?"

"Don't lose hope," she answered confidently. "When you worry, you've lost perspective. You have to keep a right mindset. I'll be back." She turned and began walking away.

"Wait!" the boy called out. "What's your name?"

She paused and spun around. "Oh, sorry, I'm Maya!" she answered. "And you are?"

"I'm Quinn."

SIXTEEN

Around midday, two armed men entered with the daily ration of food and water for both the lion and the boy. He was thankful for the provision and ate ravenously. He found it interesting that regardless of how quickly he ate, the panther ate more speedily, as if it was the last meal he would consume. Near the end of his meal, Quinn raised a bite of food to his mouth and suddenly froze mid-lift, his eyes broadening. The morsel dropped back into his plate. Did God answer my prayer from the night before? he wondered. Had God sent the girl to save me in my time of need? And why hasn't the cartel killed me yet? Was God sparing my life?

Though the room was warm and humid, he shuddered as goosebumps tingled the length of his arms. The thought of a hypothetical God who heard his prayers and answered them was too unbelievable. A God who listened to him when he had wanted little to do with him was inconceivable. If true, it confirmed that not only did a God exist, but one attainable by an immoral being. The notion of a divine Power larger than life itself incited dread within the orphan, a terror far exceeding his fear of the lion or of the armed men.

Then again, he rationalized, perhaps his prayers were not heard at all and the girl was going to show up anyway. She was the daughter of the mob leader, after all, and shots were fired yesterday. Most people would be curious and want to check it out. Of course, if there is a God, he could surely orchestrate all the events to align perfectly with the prayer of a soul in desperate need. The orphan would never know for sure, and supposed that's where the concept of faith was crucial.

The puma reassumed his routine of pacing back and forth, from one end of his cage to the other. What more would he achieve with his time? He was beyond bored and in need of exercise. He longed to be in his natural habitat, able to run and hunt alongside others of his kind to fulfill his intended purpose. Quinn joined the wildcat along the iron bars adjoining their cells. The cat stopped pacing and Quinn began stroking its fur. Every creature—every living thing—has a unique purpose, he mused.

His outlook changed that day. A happiness filled his spirit. He noticed, through distant windows across the room, new foliage turning a bright chartreuse, he felt warmth from sunshine penetrating the glass, and birds chirping outdoors. These were nothing novel, but typically went unnoticed from indifference. A dove landed on the window sill and peered inside. They stared at one another as Quinn savored the camaraderie of his feline friend. A restored hope of rescue inspired the orphan, not simply for freedom, but in spending time with Maya.

Until that time, girls to Quinn were extraordinarily ordinary, many even cute and pretty, but none of whom incited his heartbeat to race. In his soul, he knew it unreasonable for a girl to be any more ravishing than Maya. Having never received love, he was unsure what it was like, with nothing to measure it against except the lack thereof. But what he felt with this girl was closer than anything he had ever encountered. It emanated from neither lust nor unsound longing, but his rapture was drawn from the core of his being. He beheld his destiny while ensnared by her eyes, and little else presently mattered. He desired her nearness and would sacrifice everything for her affection.

Maya thirst for freedom from the lifestyle of her family. Her fondness for Quinn grew that day as he, too, longed to be set free. She hungered for the respect and genuine adoration he had shown toward her. And besides, her dreams spoke of a fate with this boy, and of him leading her to a fruitful fortune—though she dare not allude to that just yet. Together, they would realize each other's dreams and destiny. She would aid him in securing his fate as he would her own. She combed her father's manor for the key that would launch their collective journey.

That evening, Quinn wrestled with the idea of Maya not returning. Maybe she lied and gave him false hope, or perhaps she meant to return, but changed her mind later in fear of her father. His happiness from earlier that morning had quickly faded. Then he recalled someone telling him that happiness comes and goes with circumstances, but joy is deep-seated and capable of remaining despite unpleasant situations. It was a choice, he told himself. He didn't have to allow his adverse conditions to define him emotionally. He could remain in control of his mindset and outlook.

From the other side of the wall, brief muted noises awoke Quinn. It was near pitch black, but now and then he noticed the soft flicker of a flashlight around the corner. The cougar was curious, too, and stood up to observe. Suddenly, the orphan heard a faint gasp and he could tell from the glimmers of advancing light that someone was coming.

It was Maya! His heart surged and he was at once wide awake. "I searched all over the house for the key, even my father's office…and nothing. And then it dawned on me: it's probably in the same building as the cells." She inserted a key into the cell door lock. "And sure enough, it was behind the bar!" She jiggled the key a few times, but it would not turn.

"How do you know it's the right key?" Quinn asked.

"I found two; *CAGE* is written on each of them."

She inserted the second key and turned. It worked! The door unlocked and she swung it wide open. "We have to hurry!" she said in haste.

"Wait!" he cried. "Let me see the other key."

"Why?" she asked, and handed it to him.

He took the key, unlocked the cougar's cell door, and flung it open. The wild animal cautiously sauntered to the entrance and stopped, as if an invisible door existed. Quinn knelt down and pleaded, "Come on, boy, you're free!" The cat stepped through the open door and gently butted heads with the orphan. He hugged it and Maya tugged at him to get moving.

After rounding the center wall, she snatched her handbag from the bar and dropped her flashlight inside. Once outside, she paused and pulled a switchblade from her purse. She pressed a button and the razor-sharp blade sprung out instantly.

"What the——" the orphan blurted with a sudden step back and fear in his eyes.

"Relax," she whispered. "Follow me."

Quinn followed her along a dirt path beneath a canopy of trees and brush. Midway, the cougar slipped into the cover of trees and was never seen again. He would have no difficulty scaling the rock wall surrounding the compound.

Eventually the forest opened up into a cleared expanse where several Jeeps and trucks were parked. Maya crawled up to the nearest Jeep and bent down by one of the rear tires. Quinn trailed her in the secrecy of darkness and leaned in next to her. With a quick reflex, she jammed the switchblade into the sidewall of the tire. It punctured the tire effortlessly and silently. Retracting the blade, air streamed out softly and steadily. She jumped up and moved stealthily to the next truck to do the same. Quinn stared in amazement. Who is this girl? he marveled.

He shadowed her from vehicle to vehicle, until she reached the final Jeep. Instead of bending down, she inserted a key and unlocked the door. "Get in," she ordered as she climbed into the driver seat. He jumped in the other side and she started the engine. "Duck down, all the way," she added. Quinn dropped onto the front floorboard, out of eyesight, and they drove calmly down the winding driveway to the main entrance of the compound.

She stopped at the security booth at the edge of the drive and rolled down her window. An armed guard stepped out. "Where you headed?"

"Just going for a drive. I'll be back in a bit."

The guard stepped closer and peeked inside the Jeep. He shined a flashlight into the passenger side and recognized the orphan as their captive. "What's going on here?" he inquired defensively and reached for his rifle. "I can't let you go."

"It's all right," she affirmed, as Quinn reclaimed his seat. "Just open the gate."

"Your dad would kill me; it would be my life for his. You need to turn around now!" The guard pointed his rifle at them.

"Okay, okay," she pouted, and placed the vehicle in reverse. "He would never shoot at me," she mumbled while retreating. Forty yards back, she stopped the Jeep and shoved it in drive. "Buckle up," she advised Quinn. As soon as he did, she floored it, back tires squealing against the cement driveway. It was a clean break for the gate as the Jeep accelerated speedily. Quinn braced himself, clutching the door and the dashboard in front of him. In the last moment, the guard stepped out in front of them with weapon drawn. Maya slammed on the brakes, but it was too late. The vehicle plowed the armed man into the gate and burst it open with ease.

They sat there a moment in shock, and got out of the Jeep to check on the guard. Undeniably dead, they dragged his body off the drive and into the grass by the mangled gate. A commotion stirred outside the main manor and someone hollered in their direction.

"Back in the car!" Maya yelled to Quinn. Though a bit beat up and blood-stained in the front, the Jeep was in solid mechanical condition. They sped off together into the inky hue of the early morning, independent and free. Neither uttered a word. Whomever decided to chase them would soon pull over, for all remaining vehicles would have flat tires in no time.

After driving for an hour, they arrived in a small town and the sun emerged to greet the rookie fugitives. Maya pulled into an almost empty parking lot of a small grocery store and drove around to the back. She parked the battered Jeep and shut off the ignition. They sat in silence for a few seconds before Maya unbuckled her seat belt and leaned over toward Quinn. Placing her arms around him, she lay her head on his shoulder and wept. Quinn did not anticipate her intimate embrace, but had never been more enraptured in all his life. And while her affection was due to a recent traumatic incident and he barely knew her name, it mattered little. The girl he loved was in his arms and he savored every second.

"I've never killed anyone before," Maya whimpered. "Maybe I'm too much like my father."

"It was an accident," consoled the orphan. "He shouldn't have jumped in the way. What was he thinking? Who does that?"

Maya loosened her hug and withdrew from Quinn. "You don't have to continue on with me. I'd understand and wouldn't blame you."

"Are you kidding?" Quinn shot back fervently. "There's nothing that could change my mind. You saved my life; you're stuck with me!"

She wiped her face and smiled. "Okay. Then we need to get out of here."

Leaving the Jeep and its bloody grill behind, Maya tossed the keys as far as she could in a grassy field behind the store. "By the way, you should've seen your face when I pulled that knife out of my purse!" she said and laughed aloud. "You thought I was going to stab you to death. That was hilarious!"

"Laugh it up!" Quinn picked up his pace to keep up. "I don't know you that well. Maybe it was your initiation into the family business. Maybe you had to off me all on your own, and others were ready in the dark in case you botched the job. How should I know?"

She giggled while leading Quinn down a few backstreets, until they reached a hotel with which she was familiar. A cabdriver sat out front awaiting any potential customers who might need a ride from the hotel. "Perfect," she said, and they climbed into the back seat.

She directed the driver to take them in the direction from which they came, but on an alternate route entirely. "We drove the wrong way on purpose," she whispered to Quinn out of the cabbie's earshot. "That should throw them off awhile."

Quinn observed Maya sitting gracefully and delicately in the seat next to him. He was impressed by her street smarts. He wondered why he had received another chance in life and with this gorgeous girl. If only everyone obtained a second chance to righten their lives, an opportunity to alter their ways.

Studying her as she looked out the window, they caught eyes when she turned her head back around. Surely there is a God who fashioned this girl with such care and precision. There is no way, in her beauty, that she evolved from something other than a more advanced life form. Her charm materialized not by chance, he concluded.

"How old are you, anyway?" he asked.

"Sixteen…what about yourself?"

"Fifteen…almost sixteen," he promptly added.

"Oh, you're just a little baby!" she teased and tousled his hair with her hand.

He didn't mind at all and relished the attention. "So you just started driving!" he blurted while reflecting on their getaway.

THE ORPHAN DREAMER

"I actually learned when I was twelve. You're in Mexico now, you know?"

"And how do you know English so well?"

"My father wanted me to learn English at an early age. Did you know that if you learn a language before you reach adolescence, you won't be able to detect an accent?" Quinn shook his head. "My dad hired an English tutor for me; she came over almost every day. He pretty much hired somebody for everything. We had full-time maids, nannies, teachers, chefs, landscapers—you name it! Half the police officers in the area are on his payroll!"

"Oh, good, that's really comforting!" he said sarcastically.

"He's an awful man," she affirmed. "My mom moved away years ago—forced out, rather—my father could never be faithful. He had so many girlfriends. He believed it was his right and that mom was being selfish in not approving. I've been wanting to run away for a long time. You finally gave me a reason to do it now instead of waiting any longer." She turned and gazed out the window. "I'm so glad to be gone from there."

"I'm so sorry," the orphan responded.

"Oh no, nothing to be sorry about. Life is unique that way. One never knows where it will lead. What about you...where are your parents?"

A patrol car sped past them going the opposite direction, and they both looked back to make sure it didn't turn around.

Quinn averted his eyes to the back of the seat in front of him. "I never had any parents," he said, almost ashamed. "I never knew them rather."

Maya reached for Quinn's hand, tenderly intertwining her fingers with his. "Oddly, sometimes it's better that way."

123

Quinn had never thought about his unfortunate predicament like that. He inhaled deeply, slowly exhaled, and gently squeezed Maya's hand. She was absolutely right.

SEVENTEEN

Reaching the next town, Maya asked the driver to pull over. She paid the fare and they roamed a few blocks until locating another taxi cab. As they resumed their course away from the drug cartel and toward the region of the healing pool, Quinn described his dream in greater detail. He recounted the miraculous pool and how the priest at the convent paralleled a story about a similar pool from his big Book. He portrayed the scene of a Spanish armada smoldering and smoking a short distance from the cavern along the Mexican coast.

Maya listened attentively to the vision, for she believed in a spiritual realm that conveyed truths through revelation. They offered invaluable premonitions for the dreamer to use for insight and guidance. "I recall studying about the Spanish conquest in the Mexican Yucatan," she relayed. "I think it was in the 1500s. Many ships were set on fire and then sank; nobody knows for sure where they disappeared."

"Tell me again about *your* dream," said the orphan.

"I've had it several times this past year. I dreamt about a wandering boy from another country with the mark of a cross upon his face, much like yours. What I didn't mention earlier is that I was to follow him and he would lead me to great fortune."

Quinn's eyes widened as he furrowed his brow. "Great fortune?" he chuckled. "I'm pretty sure you have the wrong guy. I'm as broke as they come!"

"I shouldn't have told you," she replied. "It's silly."

Upon driving the better part of an hour, they arrived in the center of a modest-sized town. "This is good here," Maya told the cabdriver.

"Why did we get off at this spot?" Quinn asked once the cab had faded away.

"We passed a used car dealership two blocks back," she answered as she began reversing their course on foot. "I didn't want the cabbie to know we were getting a car."

Quinn was again fascinated by the resourcefulness of Maya, shrewdly blurring their trail. It would undoubtedly prove troublesome to trace their steps.

Reaching the dealership, Maya advised Quinn to wait for her out front. "It's better if they don't know you're not from around here."

So he lingered outside and observed her through the glass windows. He noticed her pointing toward a car in the lot and a discussion between Maya and the dealer. In no time at all, she drew a wad of cash from her purse and began counting. Handing it over to the man, he reciprocated with a set of keys and a handshake.

They drove off in their used Land Rover and forged ahead on their journey. "Where did you get that kind of money?" asked the orphan.

THE ORPHAN DREAMER

Maya grinned. "I may or may not have grabbed a handful of cash on my way out of my father's house. Okay, two handfuls, but that's nothing to him. He'll never miss it and he owes me anyway." That sounded awfully familiar, Quinn thought, as he reminisced his flight from the convent. He was also reminded how he repeatedly had enough in times of need, frequently just in the nick of time. Provision seemed to follow him, though he must still assume a level of initiative for his needs to be met. Laziness was never an option, he was convinced, with an expectation of provision.

Opportunity may often be discovered in the midst of an obstacle, he supposed. Though abducted, he was able to free a miserable, caged wild animal. And while imprisoned, he had met the girl of his dreams, who was now leading him to restoration in the healing pool.

Maya glanced over at Quinn. "What are you thinking about over there?"

"How situations often work out in the end, though not always how we anticipate them resolving. A person's perspective is short-sighted in the midst of suffering—there is little hope or promise. But afterwards, when things calm down and a way is made, perspective changes when you realize the bigger picture." Quinn flipped his sun visor down and examined his unruly birthmark across his face. "It's hard to believe, after all the setbacks along my trip, that I'm so close to achieving my dream. A remedy is almost within reach!"

Maya exhaled a big sigh. "Quinn, I have news for you. You have a blemish on your face. Big deal. People are flawed—all of us! Our differences, our imperfections are what connect us to humanity and validate that we're real. I love your birthmark. It makes you unique, unlike anyone else in the world."

127

"Easy for you to say," replied the orphan. "You have no flaws."

Maya roller her eyes. "Boy, don't be ridiculous…of course I have flaws!"

"Yeah? Where?"

She opened her mouth wide. "See?"

"What? I don't see anything."

Maya leaned in closer with her mouth open. "The little space in between my two top front teeth."

"Oh, come on!" Quinn snapped back. "You've *got* to be kidding. Yeah, you're hideous."

"Well, a flaw's a flaw!" she confessed. "There you have it."

"But even your imperfections are cute!" he countered.

Before leaving the town, Maya stopped the Land Rover in front of a little market. "Stay with the car. I'll be right back."

Twenty minutes later, she hopped back in the vehicle with two bags. "Right back?" challenged Quinn. "What did you get?"

She removed a tiny box and proudly handed it to Quinn.

Quinn accepted the gift with the word Jabón on top. "You got me *soap*?"

"Sorry, but you stink!" she quipped. "I mean, you *really* stink!"

Having passed a charming little river moments earlier, she circled back and parked in a secluded wooded area. The bubbling waterway was satisfying to hear as the current streamed across the smooth river rock. Emptying the remaining contents from the two bags, Maya revealed a new set of clothing for each of them, as well as hygienic supplies including toothbrushes, toothpaste, and deodorant.

"I'll go around the bend if you want to wash over there," offered Quinn.

THE ORPHAN DREAMER

"Sounds good," Maya agreed. "Don't forget to wash the clothes you're wearing, too. And no peeking or I'll kill you!" she added with an adorably sinister grin.

Later, when they both returned to the truck, Quinn couldn't believe how captivating Maya was with wet hair. "You're looking at me funny again," she said, tossing her hair around and flinging it back provocatively.

❦

Several towns later, they pulled into an old-fashioned town square in search of a place for dinner. They parked and strolled around, admiring shops and outdoor vendors peddling unique crafts and wares. A young lad, upon spotting them, ran up to dazzle them with prospects of a new customer. "Tengo un truco de magia!" the youth cried. "Aw, he has a magic trick for us!" Maya happily interpreted. They paused along the sidewalk to be charmed by his brief presentation.

The boy waved his hands melodramatically in the air before them and suddenly a shiny paper clip appeared. Extending it out with his fingers horizontally, he shook his other hand and revealed a second paper clip. Drawing it closer to the initial one, he scarcely brushed its tip and it instantly levitated in mid-air, straight out from the first. He summoned a third paper clip, and it too suspended from the second clip. The illusion was nearly foolproof, but for the hidden magnet in his hand not entirely concealed. At any rate, a valid attempt, and after securing a dollar from Maya, he extended a bow and merrily scampered away.

Discovering a charming cafe three blocks from the plaza, they rested and dined on authentic tacos al pastor, filled with

129

spit-roasted pork, onions, cilantro, and chunks of pineapple. As they ate, Maya noticed a couple sitting on the other side of the cafe. What she found notable and admirable was that they closed their eyes and prayed together once their food arrived. And while she herself was not a believer, she admired their conviction and was moved by their faith.

"That couple just prayed before eating," she told Quinn. "How inspiring that there are people who trust in a God who hears them and have the confidence to call on him in public."

Quinn agreed and proceeded to recount much of what he had learned about God along his journey. He told her about the pastor who explained how one must bow at the foot of the cross, humbly and lowly with repentance; that each must surrender to Christ as Lord. And how all are flawed internally. Many are clean on the outside, he noted, and yet their hearts are polluted inside. He revealed how Jesus often claimed that it was a person's faith that healed them. "He was speaking about physical healing," Quinn clarified, "but I'm fairly certain he was implying a spiritual cure." Quinn touched briefly on the evangelist, who insisted that people are needy—that there is a void and loneliness only God was able to fill. And that there is but one truth, not many.

Maya listened and treasured up all these truths and pondered them within her soul.

After paying for dinner, Maya asked the waiter to also charge her for the praying couple's meal. On their way out, Quinn thanked her for dinner and for all she had done for him. "And that was really thoughtful to pay for that couple. But they'll never know it was you who paid."

"Exactly," she replied. "I love doing something nice when a person will never know who did it. There's a joy, unlike any other, when you perform a good deed in secret. I'm learning it's

130

often the slight expressions of kindness that can have an enormous positive impact on other people—not to mention toward your own happiness. It's rare that a person does something for another without expecting something in return, in one way or another." Quinn found himself attracted to Maya's personality and character as he did her appearance.

On the way back to the Land Rover, shadows were lengthening as they passed a secluded alleyway. Weather-beaten brick walls on either side were neglected and severely deteriorating. But it was a sudden outcry that caught their attention. Two men were physically assaulting a third man lying on the dusty ground, trying to defend himself.

"Hey, stop!" yelled both Quinn and Maya as they ran into the back street to ward off the attackers. Ten yards from the scuffle, Maya held her arm out to hold back Quinn. "Hold on!" she ordered. One man tore the victim's jacket while trying to wrestle it from him, while the other man kicked the wounded man in the gut.

Maya pulled a shiny handgun from her purse and immediately shot straight up in the air. Quinn jumped back and dropped to the ground startled. The two muggers stopped the assault and bolted down the alley and out of sight. The gentleman was writhing on the ground, his head and arms bleeding into the dirt road. Quinn was trembling. His gaze was riveted toward Maya as she coolly replaced the handgun inside her purse. "You stay here!" she instructed. "I'll bring the car around."

Moments later, the Rover halted in the dusky alleyway. They helped the wounded man into the vehicle and zoomed off in pursuit of a hospital. The man was appreciative, and he explained that while he was being robbed, he didn't hesitate to fight back. A mistake in hindsight, he admitted, as they not only robbed him, but beat him up as well. He likely would have walked away unscathed had he simply given them what they wanted.

Upon finding a hospital, they hobbled him inside by wrapping his arms around each of their shoulders and team lifting him. What a sight he was to behold, badly bruised and bloody with clothing tattered. After explaining the assault to a nurse, he was whisked away in a wheelchair. Assured he would be well taken care of, they turned to leave, and on the way out of the lobby, they passed a policeman who watched them attentively. They climbed into their vehicle and noticed the officer had followed them outside to scrutinize their departure.

"That was crazy!" said Quinn as they drove away into the obscurity of the night and deeper into the Yucatan Peninsula.

"Which part?" Maya asked, checking her rearview mirror.

"Every part! The man getting mugged…you pulling out a gun and scaring them off! Where, by the way, did you get a gun?"

"I've had it awhile; my father gave it to me for protection. You never know when it might come in handy."

Quinn peeked inside her purse and saw the handgun. "That was impressive, I have to admit." He clutched the pistol in his right hand and bobbed it up and down delicately to gauge its weight.

"Careful, tiger," she cautioned. "I'm so tired of the depravity of mankind. Aren't you? I've been surrounded by corruption my entire childhood, and as a normal way of life at that. The

THE ORPHAN DREAMER

intentions of man are continually greedy and evil. Why can't people be kind to one another and treat others as they want to be treated? I mean, the very word *mankind* are the words *man* and *kind* combined!"

"I'm with you...it's exhausting," agreed the orphan, as he carefully returned the gun back into Maya's purse. He contemplated the immorality in the world, and how people have the free will to behave as they wish. Freedom to choose, he decided, leads many down the wrong path. Pride and wrongdoing are appealing to the self-centered soul, which invariably generates pain and suffering, confusion, and adverse consequences. "People must turn to evil when they lack the fear of God."

"So you do believe in God then?" inquired Maya.

"I didn't say that. I'm still trying to figure it all out." Quinn reflected on his journey thus far, and noticed that the more difficult circumstances actually drew him closer to God—or at least to a deeper conviction of his possible reality. When people prosper, in the absence of suffering, they are likely self-sufficient and uninterested in God, he supposed.

His mind returned to the violent assault. "You know, if we had left the cafe only one minute later, that man might have been killed."

Maya nodded her head. "Or if we had left a minute sooner, we might have missed it entirely...and he could have been killed. I do believe things happen for a reason."

"Me, too," replied Quinn, pondering the perfect timing of the incident. "Hmm."

"What?"

"I was just thinking. If that couple had not prayed before they ate, you wouldn't have paid for their meal. It was that extra minute we remained in the cafe that saved the man's life."

133

They drove for another hour with Maya checking her rearview mirror every once in a while. Few cars were on the road at all, so it was easy to tell if someone was tailing them. "Quinn," said Maya.

"Yeah?" the orphan asked.

"No, not you. We're in Quintana Roo, a state in the eastern part of the Yucatan. Does that seem odd that you were led to Quintana of all places?"

"Yes it does, but more and more, odd coincidences seem to be the norm rather than the exception. I'm becoming convinced that things don't happen by chance."

Arriving in a moderate-sized town, they stopped at a grocery store to purchase bread and snacks they could eat in the car. A street vendor selling fresh mangos caught Maya's attention and she pulled over abruptly. "I always seek out local vendors. It means the world to them and they usually offer a fresher product."

"You are a kind soul," the orphan replied.

After buying a few mangos and other goodies, they pulled into a near vacant outdoor shopping mall parking lot. "I'm going to be honest with you," Maya said. "I'm almost out of money. We can sleep here tonight. The healing pool is very close; we can go there in the morning. But after that, we should probably get jobs in town and save up for a while."

The Land Rover did not have tons of room in the back, but was spacious enough for the two of them. Lying next to one another, the orphan turned to face Maya. "Tomorrow is the day I've been destined for—the day I shall be restored."

"About that...I've been meaning to say something," she replied and shifted her body to face him also. "What if you're not healed of your birthmark tomorrow? What if nothing happens?"

134

"What do you mean? Don't you believe?" he asked, his heart disheartened. "I've had multiple dreams about renewal that will take place."

"I know. I believe in dreams, too, but sometimes visions have varied meanings. Sometimes they portray a purpose contrary to the one we perceived. I've had dreams where I was able to fly. Now, I know I can't actually fly, but maybe it alludes to something else—maybe to freedom, to persuade me to set out and take a chance, to take a risk."

With her finger, she tenderly traced his birthmark across the side of his face. Her dark chocolate eyes reminded him of the eyes of a doe, graceful and loving. She traced his beauty mark once more and then touched his lips with her finger. Grasping his hand with hers, she cuddled up close and placed her head on his shoulder. No longer could the orphan imagine life apart from this bronzed beauty lying beside him.

EIGHTEEN

In the middle of the night, they awoke to someone tapping on the window. A police officer demanded they both step out of the vehicle. "Yes, officer?" Maya asked.

"Do you not have a place to stay?" The agent shined a flashlight on them, with notable interest in Quinn's birthmark.

"We're traveling," replied Maya with a playful smirk, careful to not appear too flirty. "We only stopped for a short nap."

"Well, you can't park here. You can't sleep here, so let's move on." He studied them suspiciously, as if he recognized them but couldn't recall from where. He watched with folded arms as they climbed back into the car and casually drove away.

A few blocks down the road, another patrol car passed them driving the other direction. Due to the darkness, they were unaware it was law enforcement until the moment it passed by. They tensed up and stared down the dimly lit road behind them, watching the faint red glow of tail lights fading in the distance. A block further, Quinn noticed the tiny tail lights suddenly morph into radiant brake lights.

"He's braking!" Quinn shouted.

Maya accelerated as fast as the Rover allowed. The squad car did a U-turn in the middle of the road and flashed on its lights.

THE ORPHAN DREAMER

Still far ahead of the officer, Maya sped off, detouring hastily through town in hopes of losing him.

❧

"We lost him," Maya affirmed.

"I think you're right. But where are we?" asked Quinn.

"We made it to the site of an ancient Mayan city. This place flourished centuries ago, but was pretty much abandoned in the 1500s."

Quinn looked confused. "So what's left here?"

"Lots of ruins; it's a popular tourist attraction now. There's a castle, a couple of Mayan temples, and lots of other archaic structures." Maya opened her door and hopped out. "Come on, let's go!"

"Let's go? Go where?" asked Quinn. He could barely make out some of the obscure ruins beneath the light of the glistening moon.

"There's a cenote not too far from here."

The orphan stepped out of the Rover and closed the door. "There's a what?"

"A cenote. It means *sacred well*," she explained. "It's the healing pool you've been pursuing. We're so close!"

Maya transferred food and water, a flashlight, and her pistol and switchblade into a handbag, and together they headed into the ancient Mayan reserve. A haunting breeze swept across the plaza as age-old structures of ashen white rock soared like ghosts littered around the property. The waves of the coastline beneath them whispered gruesome secrets of a thriving people group long ago abandoned.

137

"Millions of people perished around here centuries ago from smallpox and other diseases brought over by the Spanish conquest," Maya explained. "That's the Temple of the Healing Goddess right over there," she added, pointing ahead of them.

Quinn strained to focus and identify the neglected and deserted sanctuary. "How do you know?" he asked.

"I've been here before, with friends."

"I don't think we're supposed to be here at night," Quinn said uneasily, and paused to look back. "Maybe we should leave."

Maya cupped his face with both of her hands and smiled. "Oh, we're certainly *not* supposed to be here. But we're not leaving until we locate the pool."

A pair of headlights entered the decomposing walled city of the Mayans and parked next to the Land Rover. "Uh oh," she added. A second pair of headlights trailed and parked beside the first. All lights turned off and they could barely distinguish them as patrol cars. Flashlights flicked on and examined their vehicle inside and out. The spotlights fanned out across the ruinous expanse, darting this way and that to expose any movement or foul play.

"And that settles it," mumbled Maya. "We're definitely not leaving now. Follow me!" She snuck over toward the primitive castle, El Castillo, perched high upon a bluff overlooking the ocean. For generations, it surged into the sky and faced the rising sun, to serve a lookout for seafaring vessels. It was lonely and weary now, with a spine-chilling presence in the gloomy dead of night.

They skirted around the side and rear walls of the castle, finding their way to the steep slope of steps cascading down the rocky cliff leading to the beach below. The stone staircase was a challenge during the day, she recalled from years prior, but decidedly perilous in the evening. One slip could prove deadly. With the rugged overhang screening them from the officers atop the bluff, she switched on the flashlight. They crept downward meticulously, hugging the rustic, stone stairwell.

Upon reaching the bottom, tranquil waves crashed only feet before them. The wind picked up and spoke of nautical conquests and ravaged shipwrecks. Maya led Quinn down the coastline some distance, until the rocky crag dissipated into wilderness leveling into the sea. A well-worn path jutted into the dense brush away from the water. "We're almost there," she affirmed.

Further into the jungly wilderness and the mouth of a broad cavern suddenly opened up. "This is it!" exclaimed Maya. Quinn saw the grotto and halted, and then looked at Maya. "A cave?"

"Yes," she confirmed. "The natural pond is deep within the cavern."

"I should've known there was a catch," moaned Quinn. "And in the middle of the night? Maybe we should wait until morning."

"It'll be daylight in two hours," said Maya, shining the flashlight into the giant hole. She tiptoed into the jagged rock cavern. "Besides, we can hide in there in case they come looking for us."

Quinn followed reluctantly. He remained by Maya's side for the sake of the flashlight and to maintain her balance in case she slipped. As they descended further and further into the abominable abyss, Quinn couldn't help but wonder if what awaited them below was inevitable doom. With simply the meager spotlight paving the way, the darkness closed in heavily all around. It felt as if something was eyeing them, something evil and vile and heinous who didn't approve of their intrusion. They persisted downward into the underworld, perhaps into the pit of hell itself, he imagined. Perhaps his dreams of hope were deceitful, disguising a nightmare of damnation and torment. Was this to be their fate: to die beneath the earth, their bodies to decay and abandon their souls to suffer eternal condemnation in dark and bitter solitude?

"What are you thinking about?" Maya asked.

Quinn was roused from his miserable train of thought. "Oh, nothing. Just that if we're going to die, I'm glad it'll be with you."

"I'm not going to lie, Quinn…I'm scared, too." She shined her light at a level slab of limestone adjoining the cavern wall, and sat down. "I don't know what I was thinking coming down here alone, and at night."

"Let's not go any further," the orphan suggested. "I don't need to find the healing pool. I'll be thankful if we just make it out of here alive."

"But you've come all this way. It'll all be for nothing!"

"It's okay, I don't regret a thing. I've learned so much along my journey." Quinn sat down beside her. "And I met you. I don't need a flawless face."

Suddenly, something flew into the beam of light near the lens of the flashlight. "Ahh!" Maya shrieked and swung her arm around to see what it was that swooped passed. Quinn helped her look, but the focused ray of light was challenging with the volume of darkness in sharp protest. "I think it was a bat," said Quinn. "I don't think they're that dangerous...unless they bite you...and have rabies."

"Rabies!" Maya was not relieved at all and scooted closer to Quinn on the shelf of rock. She shined the light all around the ceiling of the cave, but noticed nothing. Calming down, she took a deep breath. "No bats anywhere."

"Of course," Quinn continued, "I assume if it *does* have rabies and bites you, you either die or become a vampire."

At once, the flying creature discovered the source of the light and landed on the end of the flashlight. It was as large as Maya's hand, with walnut-colored wings and round off-white spots resembling eyes. It flapped its wings wildly, mere inches from Maya's grip. She screamed and flung the flashlight impulsively as far as she could. A ray of light spun and spiraled recklessly through the air, the beam ricocheting off the limestone walls like a strobe light. And then they heard a splash, and the light in the cavernous chamber dimmed. They crept over to the sound of the splash, and then halted in amazement.

"There it is!" said Quinn. A miniature lake of clear water with a unique beacon of light glowing in only one direction just a few feet from the surface. The flashlight had sunk to the bottom of the healing pool.

From nowhere, a colossal moth dove for the light source and slammed sharply into the water. It struggled to flap its wings to no avail. The impact onto the surface of the water was too severe, and in little time, it floated peacefully and permanently. The flashlight echoed the plight of the moth and perished soon afterwards.

The moth naturally loves the darkness, Quinn reasoned. But the insect is drawn towards light, persistently colliding into it, and yet, never comprehending the significance or purpose. In the end, light without proper discernment proved detrimental to the moth.

Moments later, the faintest hint of light from above permeated the grotto.

NINETEEN

Daylight was a welcomed sight. There's something mysterious about sunlight that lends a fresh perspective upon life circumstances. What may appear paralyzingly daunting at night somehow becomes more manageable in the daytime. A jagged hole two stories high along the cavern ceiling became visible. As sunlight intensified through the aperture, like a great flashlight shining from the top of a dome, the chamber awakened from its slumber. Rock formations resembling enormous icicles hung heavily from the ceiling. Years and years of relentless dripping of mineral deposits fashioned the dangling ornaments overhead. The cavern glistened with moisture. Some deposits trickled lazily to the ground and formed similar icicles, but in reverse, with the base upon the ground and a sharp point rising high into the air.

Sunshine illuminated the crystal clear turquoise water. It was a spectacle to behold. "Isn't it amazing?" asked Maya. "Rainwater filters down through the limestone to create the most majestic swimming pool."

"It is truly unlike anything I've ever witnessed," the orphan agreed. He stood there for some time, captivated by its natural beauty. He always believed that once he found the pool, he would immediately dive in. But things were different now, in person. The reservoir demanded respect and evoked a sense of awe from any who interfered with its serenity.

"Well, are you getting in or not?" Maya interrupted his contemplation.

"Of course," he replied, as if a burden was being abandoned for a favor. Today is the culmination of my pilgrimage, he realized. He removed his outer attire to keep them dry, and stepped into the pond in his boxer shorts. The water was brisk and pure; if ever a pool would cleanse and purify him, it was this one. He edged out until he was chest deep, his spirit inspired and animated. Maya discreetly watched him from afar. She knew it was a momentous time for Quinn, and he deserved the courtesy of time alone.

The orphan looked up and peered through the orifice in the ceiling above. "God, show me your goodness," he whispered. "Restore me...transform me, I pray." Quinn descended into deeper waters, sinking into the coolness. He remained wholly submerged for as long as he could, until at last, he pushed away from the floor of the pool and rose to the surface. Swimming back to the shallows, he stood up, inhaling and exhaling complete lungfuls of air. He felt invigorated. The chilly water tightened his skin and pores, leaving him refreshed and energized. He relaxed and allowed the reservoir to grow tranquil as it was prior to their arrival.

Soon the waters calmed and the orphan's hope heightened. He gazed downward into the surface of the water and the reflection confirmed what his heart knew would be true. The face staring back was unchanged and unaffected. He closed his eyes and realized that you cannot base reality upon your feelings. Emotions will change, and at times, may prove contrary to that which is true.

THE ORPHAN DREAMER

Wading toward the embankment, he observed the deceased moth floating in his path. He splashed to waft it aside and then withdrew from the reservoir. He dusted off another slab of limestone, and sitting down to drip dry, he noticed Maya approaching. She crouched low and embraced Quinn for some length. He hugged her back, appreciative of her concern, and finally released his grasp.

"First of all," she began. "If someone hugs you, always wait for that person to loosen their grip. The one who initiates may have the greater emotional need, so that person releases first." She smiled and continued. "Secondly, you are so handsome."

Quinn rolled his eyes. "My face didn't change at all!"

"It didn't need to," Maya insisted. "Accept it...you were made this way, Quinn! It's one of the things that makes you special. Embrace it!"

She tousled his wet hair playfully and walked away to the water's edge. Sliding her shorts off and tossing them onto a boulder within reach, she noticed Quinn watching out of the corner of her eye. She peeled off her shirt next and flung it beside her shorts, and spun around to face Quinn in her lingerie. "Don't even think about it!" she warned. "I'm waiting...and you'll have to as well," Maya affirmed as she gracefully stepped into the water.

As additional sunlight penetrated the cavern chamber from the breached ceiling, the orphan appreciated the beauty of the tiny translucent lake. The clarity and brilliant turquoise of the water was truly miraculous. He hopped off the boulder, got dressed, and wandered around the vast chamber by himself.

His hopes were dashed and his dreams had deceived him. And yet he knew it was futile. For even if he were physically restored, and though he were wealthy and had all things, it was still, in the end, all vanity. Life is damnably brief and all that

145

one accumulates remains after the spirit departs. What then is lasting? the orphan wondered. What will endure when the body is no more?

The orphan looked back toward Maya and pondered her beauty. How could anything other than an Intelligent Power have fashioned this stunning design? And while he barely knew the striking girl, he knew he was falling in love with her. Where did this emotion emanate if not from a Source superior than the creature with adoration?

He considered the craftsmanship of the vast universe and artistry brandished throughout the earth, the sky, and the sea. Something tugged at his heart, too real to ignore. One look within and his conscience condemned. He awoke to the depth of his depravity amidst the height of God's holiness—an infinite gulf intervened.

A nagging emptiness warred within his soul, impossible to ignore. He recalled what they taught in the convent: that nothing could fill the void except the One by whom it formed. God never intended man to wander the world alone. For years, the orphan wrestled with the notion, but now he knew it was valid.

Conviction overwhelmed the orphan in the dark, murky corner of the cavern. He finally understood the measure of his immorality: the bitterness, the hatred, the envy, the greed, and the lusts of his flesh. And he knew the story well, of the stain of sin upon his soul and of a God who came to save. Without blemish, he entered time and heaped all that was vile, all that was vulgar, upon himself. It's true, the orphan believed, he died for *me*. Tears streamed down the orphan's face. "I've been running from you my entire life," he prayed. "But now I recognize it is you who has pursued me. Apart from you, I am but a moth, destructive and lured in the dark."

He finally understood the scope of the death and resurrection of the Christ. He came to die for a polluted world, to become cursed for my sake. Sinless, he became repulsive, assuming ownership of every shameful act I ever committed. All my corruption was placed upon him. Disgusted with himself, and weeping in shame, he cried, "Forgive my wrongs. To you, Jesus, I surrender all that I have and all that I am. Your will be done through me."

With fresh enlightenment sprung renewed hope. Quinn's perspective was clearer, his outlook more certain and confident. And while the waters did not restore him physically, he discovered spiritual healing instead. How odd, he mused, that his birthmark and troublesome times were the means which led to his changed heart. He reminisced about his lifelong struggle of fear: with peers, with risk, with failing, and with life in general. Maybe these were no longer master over him; perhaps he could release them all and simply fear God.

He observed Maya shivering in the distance as she stepped out of the subterranean lake. Ambling back toward her, his eyes suddenly lit up, as a vivid realization swept over him. I'm no longer an orphan, he supposed, or a foundling rather, unwanted and abandoned by my parents. I have a loving Father who actually wants a relationship with me!

"What are you so happy about?" Maya asked as he drew near. "Wait, were you crying?"

"You won't believe what just happened to me," Quinn replied.

"Oh look!" interrupted Maya, gazing skyward. From the breach in the cavern ceiling, an immense butterfly gradually fluttered down overhead the crystal water. "Una mariposa; it's a blue morpho! You rarely see them." It continued to drift downward, and finding nowhere to settle along the water, it flittered closer toward Maya. She extended her arm and held out her hand. "Many people believe a wish will come true if you encounter one."

The butterfly inched closer and closer until finally perching delicately on the palm of her hand. Like the moth, its wingspan was broader than her hand. Thousands of tiny scales comprising the wings reflected shades of metallic blue. A myriad of hues from royal blue to cyan to turquoise shined radiantly in the sunlight.

"Represented by water and sky," Maya whispered now, "the color blue represents peace and healing." She was thrilled by the new arrival. "They're often a sign of new life or love." The butterfly walked a few paces, inadvertently tickling her palm. She giggled and the butterfly immediately flapped its wings and lifted into the air. They watched it elegantly flutter back through the aperture above the water and disappear.

"Wow! What are the odds?" said Maya with raised voice. "For what did you wish?"

Quinn grabbed a quick bite to eat from the handbag for the two of them. "I've been confused all my life," replied Quinn in deep contemplation. "So I wished for wisdom and discernment. What about yourself?"

Maya paused before replying. Quinn could tell she was troubled. "I wished to be free."

Quinn nodded in agreement. "And that said, we should leave before people arrive."

TWENTY

Following their path back through the grotto was much easier than their way inside. The hole in the ceiling shed sufficient light to guide them part of the way, and it wasn't long before they detected illumination from the entrance. The sun was well awake by the time they reached the entryway, and they noticed a number of tourists roaming around outside. Several guides were sporting conspicuously bright red polos with khaki shorts, so they were careful not to draw their attention. The two police officers milling about the grounds were their greatest dilemma.

"If they see us, that's it," said Quinn, hiding behind a natural boulder that had fallen perhaps centuries ago. "You'll be in trouble for a while, but your father will definitely have me killed."

"They're not going to see us," reassured Maya. "Follow me." She slipped into the brush with Quinn in her shadows. The vegetation was dense, but they only needed to circle around the main admission area and then resume along the rugged pathway that led to the sea.

Before long, the thickets and underbrush morphed and welcomed the soft, velvety sands of the beach. They rested a few minutes as the sun continued its rise in the east over the watery horizon. The ocean was absolutely breathtaking, its turquoise waters glowing with grandeur. Quinn was speechless.

Maya removed her shoes and tiptoed into the water, ankle-deep. "What are you thinking about?" she asked.

Quinn raised his arms in the air. "Look around us: the blue sky, transparent water, white sands…the lush vegetation, the ocean breeze. This didn't just happen on its own."

"It *is* unbelievable," she agreed while surveying the seafront. "It's perfect. So you think there's a grand Designer behind all of this?"

"Well, think about it," explained Quinn. "Imagine walking along this beach, and you suddenly came across a message in the sand that read, 'Jack and Diane were here!' You wouldn't think the waves moved the sand around to form the message, or that a crab shuffled around to create it. You would recognize that an intelligent life fashioned it. Right?"

"Of course," agreed Maya. "The odds are too staggering otherwise."

"Exactly! So when you look around at the complexities and designs in the world, wouldn't the rational mind again reason that only an intelligent Being could have conceived it all." Quinn looked out beyond the breaking of the surf. "Think of the moon that hangs in the sky, and how it influences the ocean currents and tides. And it serves as a nightlight in the evening for *each* side of the globe as needed! Then there's the sun: If it were just a bit closer or further away, we would all die. We have wind currents blowing clouds around to rain and water the earth...an exchange of oxygen and carbon dioxide between plants and animals and humans. What about the variety of fruits and vegetables and nuts and fish in the ocean for us to eat? Why would all of this develop on its own?"

Quinn could tell she was pondering his words. "I was going to tell you in the cave. I'm somewhat of a different person than when we arrived."

Maya looked confused. "You mean something *did* happen in the cavern pool?"

"No, not exactly. I guess I had sort of an epiphany, you might say." He had to tell her, but a part of him was nervous that she might not feel the same about him once he did. She may pull away and want nothing to do with him. He dusted the sand off the bottom of the handbag. "We should hurry in case someone comes this way."

They retreated down the coastline in the direction of the Mayan ruins, and Quinn again recounted all that he had learned on his journey and the people he met along the way. She listened to him convey the story of our separation from God on account of our immorality, and the need for a Savior who died that we might live. He explained his decision in the cave moments earlier, of his guilt and repentance, and his restored fellowship with a Father he had formerly never known.

The smooth beachfront transformed into a sandy beach with steep, rocky cliffs jutting overhead. Maya turned around and scanned the lengthy coastline to make sure nobody was following. Much of what Quinn was saying was relatable, she reflected. She, too, lacked a mother interested in her life, and had a lousy role model for a father. And the struggle to abandon her own self-absorbed lifestyle, strained with poor choices and conduct, had long convicted her. She again treasured the insights of Quinn and considered them in her heart.

TWENTY-ONE

A narrow cove opened unexpectedly within the cliff wall along the shoreline. Something lured them into the charming little inlet. It may have been the pearl white sands, powdery soft, that led them from the water's edge into the secluded alcove. It may have been the reverence of the rising cliffs on all sides of the confined corridor, or the coastal breeze nudging them deeper within the isolated nook. But whatever it was, they agreed it looked virtually unexplored for years. Up ahead, the passageway wound to the right and then shimmied to the left, and at last, the corridor broadened into a roomy expanse. The cliff walls still soared high all around with the open sky peeking through above.

"Let's rest in here a few minutes," Maya suggested. She found a wide rock, half embedded into the sand, and plopped down on top.

"Yeah," agreed Quinn, sitting beside her. "Then we can continue hiking passed this ridge and venture up and around to hopefully retrieve the Rover."

Maya patted Quinn on the leg. "And then let's get out of here! We should probably travel south a good ways. This region is too dangerous and unpredictable." She plucked two mangos from her handbag and handed one to Quinn. He took a big bite, his teeth sinking into the soft yellow amber flesh. It reminded him of the Tulum sun ascending in the sky. His parched mouth relished the sweet nectar, and being unaccustomed to eating the fruit, juice coursed down his chin.

He devoured his mango and tossed the pit toward the opposing rock wall. Maya watched the mango pit bounce against the cliff face and topple into a pile of charcoal gray rocks below. As Quinn reached for another mango, Maya dropped her half-eaten mango in the sand and gasped.

"What's wrong?" asked Quinn. "Bad mango?"

She didn't reply, but remained motionless, staring across from them, where the pit was thrown. "It's all right," Quinn assured. "It's biodegradable."

Maya pointed way above the pile of rocks, to a crudely etched cross within the charcoal-colored cliff. Engraved beneath the shelter of a cliff overhang, it was weathered and distorted, perfectly resembling the birthmark on Quinn's face. The only difference was that the inscription on the rock featured a cross, while Quinn's blemish appeared as an *X*, unless he tilted his head downward.

There was no mistaking it, and the wide open mouth on Quinn confirmed it. His eyes were riveted on the weather-beaten symbol. Not simply the fact that it was a cross, but it was too precise with every flawed detail of his own mark. "What…what in the world could it mean?" asked Quinn.

THE ORPHAN DREAMER

Maya hesitated in answering as she puzzled over the enigma. "It can only mean...that you are where you are supposed to be at this moment. The odds of you stumbling upon this are too astronomical to have happened by chance. You are here for a reason, Quinn."

Quinn ambled around the alcove and paced back and forth from one end to the other. There must be an explanation, he determined, but what? He reflected upon his dreams at the convent, regarding the healing pool and the burning ships along the coast. He recalled the people he encountered on his travels: the homeless man, the blind woman, the therapist, physician, wealthy businessman, the pastor—"The pastor!" he yelled with a sudden epiphany.

Maya had removed her handgun from the bag and was cleaning off the sand. "Pastor? What pastor?" she asked.

Quinn hurried over to Maya. "I stayed with a pastor and his wife on my way here. He kept saying, 'Your treasure lies at the foot of the cross.'" He resumed pacing before continuing. "When I crossed the Gulf, I boarded with a missionary on a ship and I thought it strange when he insisted the identical thing: 'Your treasure will be found at the foot of the cross.' And I clearly remember them each saying, 'You must bow at the foot of the cross.'"

Maya cocked an eyebrow. "What are you suggesting? There's treasure buried in that pile of rocks?" She wasn't convinced.

"I don't know what I'm suggesting," Quinn responded and moseyed over to the rock pile, scrutinizing the heap. The stones were sizable, neither huge nor small, but requiring both hands to lift each one. "But isn't it a little uncanny: the engraved cross resembling mine, the advice from those men, not to mention the fact that we just happened to enter this cove? What is the likelihood?"

155

He stared at the pile for some time, glanced around, surveyed the area, and then focused back on the pile. Finally, Quinn stooped down and picked up a rock, and then carried it well enough away and plopped it in the sand. Returning, he selected another and transferred it to his new pile. After observing him for a minute and seeing his determination, Maya accompanied him, and together they hoisted and moved the entire stack of stones. It took almost an hour, and they stopped to rest and guzzle water. They admired their handiwork and the sandy ground now exposed from the rock removal.

Quinn was inspired to forge ahead. Employing a thinly slanted stone, he dropped to his hands and knees and began burrowing in the soft sand. Admiring his ambitious spirit, Maya joined him. "Hey, didn't you say you must bow at the foot of the cross?"

Quinn paused and looked at her, and then gazed directly upward. He couldn't help but grin and then started digging faster. For over an hour they dug in the sand, when at last, they struck something solid three feet beneath the surface. Clearing the obstruction of sand revealed the lid from an ancient chest bearing an inscription from Spain. They looked at each other in astonishment, and then immediately trenched more deeply around the perimeter of the lid. Several inches further, they exposed a corroded lock and latch which both crumbled upon grasping.

Together, they carefully and gradually lifted the lid. Propping it onto the open chest, they tilted it against the wall of sand inside the excavated hole. Thousands of gold coins, untouched by human hands or the light of day for centuries, stared back at them. Embedding their hands into the coins, they scooped them up and allowed them to spill through their fingers and clink upon the ones beneath.

After an extended speechless moment, Maya finally broke the silence. "I...I can't believe..." she stammered. "How is this possible?"

"I don't know. But it's way too heavy to carry," said Quinn. "And there's no way to get the Land Rover down here." He looked around at the sand and steep cliffs.

"We'll definitely need a boat," Maya agreed.

"Yeah," said Quinn, surveying the hole before them. "Let's cover it back up and return tomorrow."

After burying the chest beneath a couple of feet of sand and half as many rocks, the sun was sinking and they were worn out. They polished off their remaining food and took a quick dip in the ocean to cool down. Then they dried in the coastal breeze and lied upon the powdery sand within the shelter of the cove.

"Now we can go anywhere we want," said Maya. "It's like a dream come true."

"It *is* a dream come true, literally," agreed Quinn. "Tomorrow, everything will be different."

Through the portal among the towering cliff walls, they contemplated the stars overhead. "The stars are like the heavenly host," proposed Quinn. "The sun sheds light for all to see, and even the moon, to reflect the glow of its light in the darkest of times."

Maya yawned as she allowed her imagination to wander the boundless span of the universe. "Imagine if the stars were blank canvases for the children of God to one day design a world of their own beneath his sovereign rule. Think of the unique plants and animals, terrains, and water features...the possibilities would be infinite. Quinn?"

The faint snoring of Quinn was drowned by the endless crashing of tranquil waves nearby.

TWENTY-TWO

"Despiertan!" ordered the policeman as he kicked Quinn's foot. "Wake up!"

Quinn and Maya awoke to four police officers blocking the exit to the cove. "Get up!" the same agent commanded. They searched their handbag and confiscated the pistol and switchblade. Both were handcuffed and escorted down the beach and over a ridge to a couple of parked patrol cars. After being ushered into the back seat of one of the squad cars, it hustled off in a hurry.

"That's it," said Quinn. "Your dad will kill me."

"We've come so far; don't give up now," reassured Maya. "My papa always wanted me to be brave. He said that even if you're scared, act as if you're not. People are easily fooled."

❦

Entering the cell was like déjà vu from his time at the cartel compound. It was warm and muggy, and the room heartless and sterile. His cellmate was welcoming as he rose from his bed to greet the newcomer. Carpeted in tattoos, he was a stout man with shaved head, and appeared utterly incapable of joy. Quinn wondered about the two teardrop tats below his left eye. The convict spoke a few incomprehensible words in Spanish and then shoved Quinn into the cell bars.

It wasn't worth retaliation, Quinn decided. The offender was merely staking claim to his territory, even if only a confined cell...not to mention, he would certainly suffer defeat in a brawl. And yet, Quinn was not so fearful of him and his dread of Maya's father was lessening. He had little to fear any more—the thought of death was losing its sting. What he faced were momentary light afflictions, he told himself, and they would soon pass. Even if he is executed, he could face it now.

Quinn observed Maya being led away from a different cell, and learned that she was allowed to leave. They certainly knew of the stolen car and of the man they inadvertently killed upon their escape from the mob. Plus, he was the foreigner; he would take the fall and suffer the punishment for their actions. He was doomed unless Maya could talk her father into granting him grace.

Reflecting back, he noticed that the closer he arrived in his pursuit of his dream, the more threats and challenges surfaced. From a fallen tree on the train tracks, a charging bull, being chased by a witch, running out of money, and being kidnapped, roadblocks continually emerged as he neared his calling. Now he faced jail time with dashed hopes for survival, and yet, he surprisingly had never felt more free in all his life. An indescribable calmness filled his soul.

Quinn attempted to build a silent rapport with his cellmate, for neither comprehended one another verbally. Likening it to his encounter with the mountain lion, the criminal was comparable to the wild cat in desperate need of compassion and kindness. Quinn determined to seek the good in people and to be slower to judge. He didn't know the man's entire story: perhaps he is innocent or he had a gruesome childhood with little opportunity. Or maybe his wrongdoings were justified as his own were warranted in escaping the cartel.

Quinn kneeled on the floor, leaned over his cot, and quietly prayed for Maya, for his cellmate, and for his own welfare. As Quinn bowed his head, his bunkmate perceived his birthmark forming the image of a cross. When Quinn noticed him watching, the man angrily fashioned the sign of the cross by intersecting his two index fingers. He then strutted over to Quinn's bunk and grabbed his pillow; he would have two pillows now.

This went on for several days, until one evening, while lying in bed, Quinn heard his new friend praying faintly. The hulking man was kneeling in the corner, in the dark, and sobbing. Unable to understand his prayer, he did repeatedly hear him utter the phrases, "Dios mío, lo siento" and "Perdona mis pecados".

God wants to transform an individual from within, Quinn mused. Whether a person is outwardly angry or joyful, you never really know for certain what is going on inside. But Quinn was learning one thing for sure: that all are needy, even the one who seemed least likely.

While bodily healing Quinn had not found, he did both emotionally and spiritually, far more crucial than anything physical, he now recognized. And as no two fingerprints are alike, each person is unique. God desires him to be distinct from others, set apart, that he might use him in extraordinary ways in drawing others to himself.

He was reminded of the boy with the magnetic magic trick in the town square, and conceived a similar relationship between God and man. Since man is corrupt, a holy God is unable to enjoy close fellowship with him apart from his Son. God is repelled from the presence of sin. When a man genuinely repents, though, there is a new chemistry, and like a magnet, a restored gravitational drawing toward God. Living apart from God and his ways is like facing similar poles on two magnets toward each other. Repulsion occurs and the magnets repel from one another. It was all making sense, and almost hinted of the solar system, with its healthy magnetic field, where all is aligned and properly functioning: the earth, the moon, and the sun.

A week after being incarcerated, the cell door opened and Quinn was free to leave. He learned that they thought he had beaten and robbed the elderly man from the neighboring town. Bystanders heard gunshots, which seemed to match the handgun in their possession. And eyewitnesses described the getaway vehicle and car occupants, and it all matched. Quinn breathed a sigh of relief. They had no idea about them plowing into the cartel member with the Jeep, and Maya's father still had no clue where they were!

The burly cellmate offered few words on Quinn's way out, but he extended a warm handshake. While still rugged and intimidating, his eyes were welcoming and somehow softer now. Upon entering the front lobby of the police station,

THE ORPHAN DREAMER

Quinn noticed a refined and affluent gentleman grinning, sporting bandages and an arm sling. It was the man they helped in the alley one week prior. The gentleman hugged Quinn heartily. "Thank you for saving my life back there."

Quinn smiled back. "Thanks for getting me out of jail!"

The man replied, "Someone is looking out for us. You see, you either possess the favor of God or you don't. That's not to say all will go your way, for certainly it won't. And yet, if a person is in his favor, all things work toward his good—even the bad events in your life. Not so if one is outside his favor, though. One is either under his protection or he is left out on his own."

Quinn understood what he was saying. It seems there is always a reason things happen—some good, some seemingly bad—but even the bad must serve a purpose in design, be it reproof, or warning, or in altering one's behavior. "It's almost like karma, with God being the karma," Quinn added. "You reap what you sow."

"Precisely." The polished man reached out and gave Quinn an envelope. "Don't open it until we part. I wish you well, young man."

The gentleman left in his car and Quinn strolled down the road in the opposite direction. It was a magnificently beautiful day, Quinn noted as he savored the fresh air and felt the warmth of the sun on his face. A devastating storm makes a sunny day that much more dazzling, he realized. And there was something about sunshine that brightens the spirit and revives hope. I never wanted to be kidnapped, he reasoned, but I met Maya as a result. His cellmate flashed before his mind. I didn't want to go to jail, and yet a hardened man was possibly changed from his influence. I never wished to be an orphan, abused and neglected, and yet, my Father now burns more

163

radiantly than had I never endured my adversity. Much was due to my hideous birthmark, he determined. He despised the blemish, but it was his flaw which led him to God, which attracted his soulmate, and lured a soul to Christ.

Quinn paused and opened the envelope to find a bundle of cash. His face beamed as provision honored him once again undeservedly. He stumbled across a post office, where he purchased an envelope and several stamps. And with a bit of the money just received, he added a note and sealed the envelope. Remembering the mailing address well, he addressed it and left the return address blank. He wanted to set things right, to restore the cash he stole from the convent, even though he struggled to forgive their abuse. He knew grudges were as poison in the body, and with forgiveness, grief was released. He hoped, in time, even his bitterness would diminish.

TWENTY-THREE

A bustling little taco cart on the side of the street seduced the boy near. Smells of grilled chicken, onions, and roasted red peppers wafted through the air tempting those who passed by. He ordered three street tacos, found a bench, and sat down to feast. It seemed so long since he had enjoyed a good, authentic meal. He took a long gulp of soda and his thoughts began to swirl.

He had been in jail for a week. Would he be too late? Maybe Maya couldn't be trusted. Had he been naive and simply used by her to locate the chest? Perhaps she returned to the alcove and took the treasure for herself. The possibility churned in his gut, and he lost his appetite.

Giving away his last fajita taco, he entered a local shop and purchased an assortment of foods for later. On his way out, he asked the cashier where he might acquire a small boat.

❧

Quinn hiked toward the beach, and before long, he spotted a dealer of both new and used boats. And while there was a wide variety, the entire collection was meager. But at last, one caught his attention he could not refuse. It was stylish and flaunted a certain romantic charm, and it fit nicely within his price range: a vintage mahogany inboard runabout boat named *La Mariposa*, tastefully painted in the stern.

The vendor included two anchors, a pair of life jackets, a full gas fill up, and a crash course on boating. It turned out to be much simpler to operate a boat than Quinn had imagined. And so, with his supplies, he headed out into the sea, hugging the coastline, in search of the esteemed alcove.

Night was falling as he discovered the sandy inlet snaking into the rocky cliffs. Shadows were a thing of the past for the day. Quinn creeped up to the shore as discreetly as possible and plunged the bow anchor into the shallows. He then tossed an anchor off the stern and firmly tightened it up. The boat wasn't going anywhere.

Quinn hopped into the clear, shallow water and trudged through the sand leading into the secret nook. His heart began to race as he anxiously wondered what awaited him within. Would there be an empty hole, where once the ancient trunk was buried? Had Maya seized it all and simply abandoned him?

Rounding the final curve in the craggy corridor, he noticed a figure lying on a couple of blankets in the sand. The heap of rocks was undisturbed, precisely as they had left them. He inched nearer, striving to recognize her in the dark shades of gray permeating the hidden den.

It was her! His eyes watered as he beheld Maya peacefully sleeping. She was even more stunning than before. He lied down beside her and gently stroked her hair. She awoke with a jolt, but immediately her inner longing was aroused. "Quinn!" she cried, grabbing him and pulling him close. She locked lips with his, her tongue impassioned and tasting like honeyed mango.

"I kept checking on you," she said, "but they wouldn't let me see you."

"There was good reason," assured Quinn. "All in perfect timing and according to plan."

The canopy of night was dense beyond the sea and rising ridge. Stars gleamed against the onyx sky within the window of open air above them. Quinn noticed the Orion constellation peeking between the surrounding cliffs, and pointed it out to Maya. The great Hunter, perpetually in his eternal pursuit. He now believed that he was allured to the stability offered by the stars. They were reliable, predictable, and ever unchanging. His entire life, he realized, expressed a deep yearning for stability.

"Well, I suppose my dream came true after all," said Maya with a sense of fulfillment in her voice. "Foretelling of a boy who would lead me to great treasure."

"It's almost inconceivable," Quinn added, "to have found a forsaken trunk filled with Spanish coins after hundreds of years."

Maya turned and looked directly in his eyes. "I grew up around money my whole life; it never satisfies. I wasn't referring to the chest, Quinn. While I waited for you, I considered your words from before. I entrusted my life to Christ as you. It is God whom I treasure…and you, of course."

Quinn's eyes teared up again, and he marveled at the softening of his spirit. Maya wiped a tear from his cheek. "You're stuck with me, boy—forever."

Forever sounded fine with me, thought Quinn. He glanced once more at Maya lying beside him and couldn't help but smile before closing his eyes. Recounting all the good that had happened to him along his journey, he imagined a guardian angel perched high upon the moon peering down and watching over them as they slept.

TWENTY-FOUR

Quinn awoke sluggishly to the gentle, methodical sound of beeping. He opened and closed his eyes several times before a woman rushed in and stopped the dinging. She hovered over him with a broad smile and said something, though what he was unsure.

Who was this lady? he wondered. And where am I? He opened his eyes wider and looked around. A window ushered in rays of sunlight on his right side; a white curtain clinging to the ceiling hung a few feet to his left.

"How are you feeling today?" he heard the lady ask. Another woman scurried in and began shuffling things around beside him.

"Can you hear me?" she inquired. "You're okay. Just relax, everything is all right."

A doctor carrying a notepad heroically entered the sterile room. "Well, look who's awake!" he exclaimed with an impressive smile.

"You gave us quite a scare," one of the nurses added in a motherly tone. "You've been out for two days." She checked Quinn's vital signs on his monitor and fluffed a pillow.

The physician approached closely and examined Quinn's left eye. "You took quite a hit to the head. They say the convent wall has a nice dent to prove it," he quipped. "Other boys your age can be rather ruthless sometimes, I'm afraid." The doctor shifted to inspect his right eye. "Someone must be looking out for you!"

After a slew of tests, the doctor's confidence heightened. "Everything looks good," he assured Quinn. "We'll keep you here a couple of more days for observation and further testing, but after that you should be free to go!"

The doctor left the room and a nurse approached. "I'm Maya. If you ever need anything, just ask."

"Maybe one thing," inquired Quinn. "Would you happen to have a writing pad I could scribble on?"

"Of course!" she replied, and off she went. In no time, she returned with a new spiral notebook. "Now don't hesitate. If you need anything else, you can hit this button if I'm away and I'll come running."

That evening, Maya helped a patient on the other side of the drawn curtain to gather his belongings so that he might leave the hospital. His parents helped their young son settle into a wheelchair and they promptly wheeled him away out of the room and down the hall.

The curtain divider was slid all the way to one wall, enlarging the room to twice its size. "You have the room all to yourself now, Quinn," Maya said while tidying up the newly vacant space.

"Excuse me…Maya," Quinn broke his silence. "I'm a bit confused."

Maya stepped closer and sat in an adjacent chair. "That's completely normal under your circumstances, hun. Most people are pretty disoriented when they come around. It would be odd if you weren't, to tell you the truth."

Quinn peered out the window into the darkening sky. "I had the craziest dream. I met a girl whose name was Maya."

"Oh, I'm much too old for you, honey," the nurse laughed. "You likely heard someone call me that while you were under. The mind can play tricks on you sometimes."

"But the dream went on and on," Quinn persisted unconvinced. "It was so involved and so real; I was sure that it happened."

"Well, if you ask me," Maya explained, "dreams are like a window allowing the spirit world to brush alongside the physical." She sat back and thought for a moment before nodding as if she had received more enlightenment. "It's as if a portal is opened, just briefly and with limits, of course, permitting a connection between the two dimensions." The nurse studied her patient for his reaction. "When we sleep, and while you were in a coma, we are basically unconscious for a time, and yet our spirit remains somewhat alert and active with the spiritual dimension."

Quinn pondered her words.

"That's my understanding anyway!" Maya blurted when she noticed him mulling over her theory. "I may be way off, but that's how I see it." She rose from her chair and began straightening and tucking in his sheet around him. "Now you rest up and I'll be back to check on you."

She set a few periodicals on a rolling table beside the bed. Quinn glanced over, and his attention was immediately drawn to the journal on top. It was a travel magazine showcasing the coastal town of Veracruz on its cover. "Just in case you get bored," she said warmly.

"Oh no!" she suddenly cried on her way to the door. Something had caught her eye beneath the empty adjacent bed. Stooping down, Maya reached underneath and grabbed it: a small stuffed animal. "He forgot his lion!" She placed it tenderly upon a shelf along the front wall of the room. "We'll keep it here for now. They'll come back for it."

That evening, Quinn rested alone in his room, except for the occasional nurse filtering in and out to check his vitals or deliver food and drinks. The open blinds lent a limited view of the few stars dotting the sky. He thought about Orion and speculated where the constellation might be visible. In the dim lighting of the hospital suite he felt the stare of the stuffed mountain lion upon him. Its gaze penetrated the boy's eyes and deep into his soul. What were the odds of the stuffed animal being left behind, and furthermore, on it being a lion? he wondered. He sensed a manner of protection under the cougar's watchful guard.

Sleep was inducing him to the other side with a heaviness. Quinn ran his arms and hands beneath the blanket and nestled his head into the soft pillow. In spite of being stuck in a hospital and hooked up to a machine, he considered, it was the most comfortable bed he had ever slept in.

THE ORPHAN DREAMER

Two evenings and the better of two days following, Quinn packed his bag of extra clothes and random items the convent had dropped off earlier in the week. Maya led her patient down several lengthy corridors and toward the front entrance. He was free to leave and a taxi would be awaiting him.

The fresh air brushed his face and his senses animated. "What a gorgeous day to be alive!" exclaimed a woman seated upon a bench near the sliding exit doors.

"You can say that again," Quinn replied, contemplating that he could have died in the hospital. He observed the lady's sunglasses and cane and knew she was blind as she faced his general direction with a beaming smile. "How do you—" he stopped himself, recalling his dream. The woman's other senses were heightened, he knew, with the loss of her eyesight. What delight a person may possess in light of misfortune. It *was* a wonderful day to be alive, he agreed. He would be sure to make the most of it.

"Enjoy your afternoon!" he hollered back while clambering into the front seat of the awaiting cab. The cabdriver extended a curious look, unaccustomed to passengers in the front seat, but then he grinned and began pulling away from the hospital.

Quinn couldn't believe they were heading back to the convent. Oh, how he dreaded it there! At least it provided food and a roof over his head; maybe it wasn't so bad after all.

His dream had been so meticulous and lifelike. And while dangerous, even horrifying at times, it had been an adventure. He had tasted freedom; it seemed anything was possible.

He flipped his sun visor down and flipped open the mirror. The rectangular glass was cracked precisely down the center, a clean vertical fracture, as if intentionally allotted so. His birthmark stared back relentlessly. It could be worse, Quinn mused. He should be thankful.

173

Flicking the sun visor back up, Quinn noticed an enormous billboard approaching, advertising a travel service. A young woman resembling the girl from his dream was strolling along a pristine sandy beach beaming with joy, and a caption next to her read, "Follow Your Dreams!"

The sign flew past in a moment and moved Quinn to reflect upon his visions while in the hospital: wandering down the white sands of the Tulum shoreline with a girl as lovely as the one in the ad. What was the likelihood? Was it simply a coincidence? He missed her deeply now, even while never really having met her. How strange life can be at times.

The cabbie also noticed the billboard, and perceiving the deep thoughts of his passenger, decided to reassure the boy. "Hey, we each possess a special calling in life," he began slowly. "We were meant to do extraordinary things."

Quinn wasn't sold. *He's a cabdriver—what could he possibly know about special callings in life? And I'm a poor kid, a nobody.*

"Don't stress over it," the driver continued, seeing the boy's skepticism. "Just do the right thing and you will be certain. The clouds will lift and your heart will lead you in the way you should go."

"Will it always know?" Quinn interrogated the man with curiosity. *It wouldn't hurt to play along.*

"The conscience is an internal guide," he replied with certainty. "It advises between right and wrong, between good and evil. But never forget: the more one ignores its instruction and warning, the more numb it grows. That's what permits the fog and confusion to drift and settle within."

The cab parked in front of the convent and Quinn grabbed his bag and said farewell to the driver. He paused on the curb as the car receded down the avenue. After gazing into the distance and surveying the setting sun, he began the descent toward the convent's veranda. A jagged branch had broken away and now contorted across the shadowy path. It reminded him of the tree that had fallen across the train track in his dream, and he briefly laughed aloud at the parallel incident.

Stepping over the broad limb, he meandered toward the front door. A blue butterfly settled directly before him on the bronze doorknob. Quinn froze and examined the welcomed intruder, remembering that the blue morph was a good omen. Happiness and great fortune often followed such a sighting, some insisting the occasion was a rare chance in making a wish.

Moments later, the butterfly fluttered off and Quinn watched it wander away in the direction of the remote bus station, beyond the reach of the eyes. Quinn considered his present plight: he had no money and no possessions except the belongings in his bag.

After a trance-like stare off into space, he glanced back at the door, grabbed the knob, and tried to turn it. It was locked. It was always locked. If only he had family somewhere, he reasoned. But he did not and he knew so few beyond the confines of the convent.

Oh, how he wished his dream had been real! Quinn's eyes watered as he reminisced his adventure that transformed his life…or so he had believed. If only Maya were present with him now. He longed to see her again, if simply for a moment.

He glimpsed back to where he lost sight of the butterfly only seconds earlier. It could be anywhere by now. Time had a way of separating the present from the past, Quinn realized, if purely in the passing of an instant. An opportunity could be forfeited forever in a split second.

Quinn gripped the door knocker and tapped gently on the door. He wiped his brow. Darkness was quickly gaining. He was certainly too young to venture off on his own. What choice did he have? His heart was racing. Again he knocked, more heavily this time, with thoughts conflicting, more anxious than before.

Two porch lights switched on and the door lock was unlatched with a heavy metallic clink. A gray-haired woman unhurriedly drew it open half-way, and then fully. Cautiously, she hobbled outside beneath the glow of the sconces and peeked around. "Hello?" she whispered in the breeze.

She squinted her eyes and scanned the front courtyard. "Hello!" she demanded. "Who's out there?"

A tiny shadow darted and something fluttered swiftly above the old lady. She twisted her neck to see, but looked away as the light of the porch was much too offensive. It was simply a moth, delighted by the curious new source of light illuminating the portico. Flying haphazardly, it continued to collide against the glass fixture.

"Damn you kids!" the gangly woman yelled into the deserted night. Shuffling back inside, she slammed the door shut and slid the lock sharply into place with a smack.

After settling in near the back of the bus, Quinn noticed something protruding from in-between the seat and the back seat rest. He pulled it out carefully—a twenty dollar bill! That would come in handy, he was certain. He stuffed it into his pocket and scribbled an idea into his notebook from the hospital. Then setting it down on the seat beneath the glow of the moon penetrating the far window, the young aspiring writer drifted anxiously to sleep.

Made in the USA
Las Vegas, NV
24 January 2024

84842347R00111